EGYPT AND MESOPOTAMIA

Published in 1996 by
Marshall Cavendish Corporation
99 White Plains Road
Tarrytown, NY 10591-9001
U.S.A.

Editor: Henk Dijkstra
Executive Editor: Paulien Retèl
Revision Editors: Ben Haring (Earliest History of Egypt, The Middle Kingdom,
The Mighty Empire of Egypt, The Fall of the New Kingdom),
Frits Naerebout (The Minoan Civilization, Mycenae),
Henk Singor (The Sumerians, Akkad and the Sumerian Renaissance,
Hammurabi and Gilgamesh, Babylon, Assyria)
Art Director: Henk Oostenrijk, Studio 87, Utrecht, The Netherlands
Index Editors: Schuurmans & Jonkers, Leiden, The Netherlands
Preface: Megan Cifarelli, Ph.D., Fellow, Department of Near Eastern Art,
The Metropolitan Museum of Art, New York
Translated by: EuroNet Languages Services, Inc. New York, NY 10018

The History of the Ancient and Medieval World is a completely revised and
updated edition of *The Adventure of Mankind.*
©1996 by Marshall Cavendish Corporation, Tarrytown, New York,
and HD Communication Consultants BV, Hilversum,
The Netherlands

Library of Congress Cataloging-in-Publication Data

History of the ancient and medieval world / edited by Henk Dijkstra.
p. cm.
Completely rev. and updated ed. of :The Adventure of mankind (second edition 1995).
Contents:—v.2. Egypt and Mesopotamia.
ISBN 0-7614-0353-1 (v.2).—ISBN 0-7614-0351-5 (lib.bdg.:set)
1. History, Ancient—Juvenile literature. 2. Middle Ages—History—Juvenile literature. I. Dijkstra, Henk. II. Title: Adventure of mankind
D117.H57 1996
930—dc20/95-35715

History of the Ancient & Medieval World

Volume 2

Egypt and Mesopotamia

Marshall Cavendish
New York Toronto Sydney

Egypt and Mesopotamia

The three pyramids at Gizah, Egypt

CONTENTS

Preface

The ancient civilizations of the Egyptians, the Minoans and Mycenaeans in the Aegean world, and of the Mesopotamians in the Near East developed independently, yet none were fully isolated. People traveled freely by land and sea in the ancient world over enormous distances, some seeking a new homeland, others as merchants, seamen, diplomats, warriors, and prisoners of war. Along these routes, raw materials and manufactured products were transported, as were languages, customs, and even religions.

Of these cultures, the ancient Near East, particularly the region in modern Iraq called Mesopotamia by later Greek conquerors, was the earliest. It is the birthplace of true "civilization," usually defined as the development of agriculture, technology, complex social organizations, urbanization, and writing. Mesopotamian society was shaped by millennia of migrations and invasions of foreign peoples, whose new languages, religions, and cultures enriched and strengthened local traditions. The thriving and colorful cultures of the Sumerians (3400-2000 BC), Akkadians (2334-2158 BC), Assyrians (ca. 2000-612 BC) and Babylonians (ca. 1800-539 BC) had deep impact not only on the development of the ancient Near East, but on the course of western civilization. Perhaps the most important contributions of Mesopotamia were the development of written documents, kingship, sciences such as mathematics and astronomy, modern warfare, epic literature, and political and religious art.

The early development of Egyptian civilization was parallel to that of Mesopotamia, yet its unique geography and climate caused its culture to evolve along a radically different path. For most of Egypt's history, because of its dependence on the Nile River and the harshness of the surrounding land, its people were relatively isolated and its culture developed free of foreign influences. These circumstances gave rise to a conservative culture that focused its energy and resources on the glorification of the gods and goddesses, and of the god on earth, the pharaoh. The greatest monuments of ancient Egypt, such as the Great Pyramids of Giza from the Old Kingdom, and the Tomb of Tutankhamen from the New Kingdom, are characterized by this fusion of royal and divine symbolism.

In the early second millennium BC, when the civilizations of Egypt and Mesopotamia were already fully developed, two new and vibrant cultures were emerging in the region of modern Greece. The Minoan civilization of the Mediterranean island Crete, which peaked around 1500 BC, created impressive palaces decorated with sumptuous paintings that reveal a great love for life, nature, and ceremony. A century later, the more warlike Mycenaean civilization of the Greek mainland dominated the Mediterranean world. These sophisticated and lively cultures would disappear in the so-called Dark Age of Greece, but references to them in Greek mythology, legends, and literature testify to their lasting appeal.

Megan Cifarelli, Ph.D.
Fellow, Department of Ancient Near Eastern Art
The Metropolitan Museum of Art, New York

View of the Nile Valley in Egypt. When this river overflowed, which it did each spring, fertile silt was deposited. As a result, irrigation and agriculture became possible.

Earliest History of Egypt

Divine Pharaohs Unite the Country and Lead It to Prosperity

Hundreds and even thousands of years before the birth of democracy in classical Greece, the extraordinarily complex civilizations of the ancient Egyptians, the Minoans, and Mycenaeans in what is now Greece, and the ancient Mesopotamians living in the region of modern Iraq were flourishing. People from these lands were often in contact with each other, exchanging ideas, customs, goods, and language. These cultures had many features in common, such as deep religious beliefs, dependence upon powerful centralized governments and rulers, and desire to produce and be surrounded by richly decorated, beautifully crafted buildings and objects. Nonetheless, the geography and climate of each region—the isolation of

Egypt, the coastal position of Minoan and Mycenaean settlements, and the great crossroads of Mesopotamia—gave rise to the unique characteristics of these civilizations.

Lying in northeast Africa, Egypt today is largely desert country. The part of it fit for human habitation has always been far smaller than its total area. The Libyan Desert, part of the Sahara, lies in the west, the Nubian Desert to the south, and the Arabian (or Eastern) Desert borders on the Red Sea and the Gulf of Suez in the east. Across them to the north lie the desert and the mountains, rising 7,000 feet (2,133.6 meters), of the Sinai Peninsula. The only habitable territory is a narrow strip of fertile ground along the Nile River, its delta, and several large desert oases.

The Nile is one of the longest rivers in the world. From its source in the Kagera River, it drains into Lake Victoria in east central Africa and then flows north to the Mediterranean over 3,470 miles (5,583 kilometers). Called the White Nile south of Egypt, it joins the Blue Nile at Khartoum (in Sudan). Both are named for the color of the water. The Blue Nile carries rich black sediment from the Ethiopian Highlands. Deposited in the Nile Delta, a fan-shaped plain some 155 miles (249.4 kilometers)

Egyptians hunting for
fish and birds in the swamps
along the Nile.
Relief from a grave of the
fifth dynasty,
around 2400 BC

wide on the Mediterranean coast, it makes the region the most fertile in the country. The Nile Valley is narrow in Egypt, only 2 to 14 miles (3.2 to 22.5 kilometers) wide, and lined by cliffs. Navigation between Khartoum and Aswân (on Egypt's southern border) is difficult because of a series of cataracts, or rapids. The rainy season in central Africa causes the water level to rise as much as twenty-three feet (7 meters). Before the completion of the Aswân High Dam in AD 1971, the Nile would overflow its banks, leaving a fertile layer of silt on the land as it went down.

Herodotus, the Greek historian who visited Egypt in the fifth century BC, thought the repeated deposits of river mud were so essential that he regarded the country as a gift of the river. The Aswân High Dam, although creating the huge Lake Nasser reservoir (3,000 square [4,827 kilometers]

miles), has reduced that annual gift of silt as it has the flow of the Nile. Salt water from the Mediterranean has entered the delta and eroded the land.

The Country and Its Earliest Inhabitants
The earliest traces of settlements in Egypt date from the seventh millennium BC when North Africa had a less arid climate. Found in the southern desert regions, these settlements support evidence from about 4500 to 4000 in the Nile Delta showing that the earliest Egyptians grew barley and wheat and baked bread. They also kept animals, hunted, fished, and gathered wild plants and fruits. Around 4500 BC, as agriculture became more prevalent and production of food more regular, lifestyle changed in Egypt's Predynastic cultures. Larger communities permitted greater distribution of labor, evident in the production of pottery and tools made of copper in addition to flint. The Arabian Desert was of considerable economic importance, rich in lead, tin, copper, gold, semiprecious stones, and in granite and sandstone used for building.

Egypt's independent historical development and the unique culture characterizing it for thousands of years can be explained, in part, by its self-sufficiency and relative isolation.

Contact with Neighboring Peoples
Nevertheless, Egyptians were not totally isolated from other cultures. Influences from western Asia can be detected in evidence of plants and animals domesticated there earlier than in Egypt. Certain types of pottery decoration common in western Asia were adopted by the Egyptians around 3000 BC. The cylinder seal, popular in Mesopotamia, was introduced then. It is also possible that Mesopotamia, which had already developed writing, influenced the pictorial writing system called hieroglyphics that developed in Egypt about this time.

Archaeologists have distinguished several cultures from Egypt's Predynastic period (4500–3100 BC) named after the sites where they were discovered: Badarian, Amratian (Naqada I), and Gerzean (Naqada II and III).

Linguistic uniformity probably did exist, at least by the end of prehistoric times. Egyptian, the language of Egypt from its ancient times, was replaced by Arabic about the fourteenth century AD. Egyptian and its descendent, Coptic, have five thousand years of recorded history, the longest of any language. Classified as Hamito-Semitic, it is related both to Semitic languages like Babylonian, Hebrew, and Arabic, and to African languages and Berber. Assumed to have developed long before the appearance of writing, it has very different spoken and written forms.

The Kingdom of Egypt

The Nile Valley is divided geographically and culturally into two regions, Lower Egypt (the northern delta) and Upper Egypt in the south. The inhabitants of the delta had frequent contact with neighboring people; new groups usually entered the country from the Mediterranean and the Sinai. The southerners were more isolated and more conservative. By about 3200 BC, these communities were consolidated into a united kingdom under one king.

The earliest-known hieroglyphic writing dates from this period (ca. 2950 BC). A stone pallet depicts a ruler of Upper Egypt named Narmer, who conquered the inhabitants of the delta. Later Egyptian and Greek chronicles mention Menes as the first king and founder of the capital of Memphis. Whether Narmer and Menes were the same person is uncertain, but the unification of Egypt may well have resulted from the south conquering the north. Some historians cite an 0 dynasty with some thirteen rulers, ending with Narmer in 2950.

The Archaic Period: 3100–2755 BC

The available texts give little information about the early kingdom. Archaeological material can be supplemented by data from the chronicles of later kings, especially the

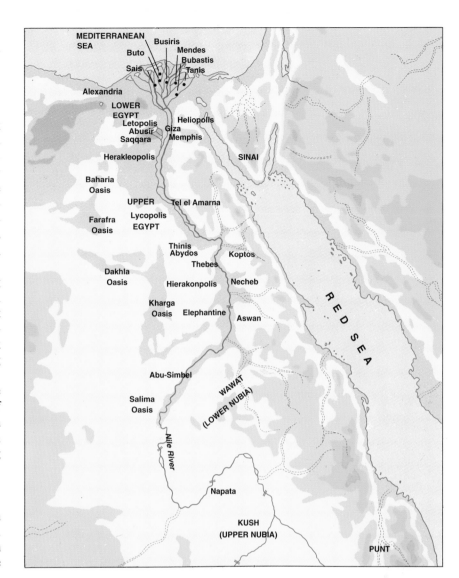

Map of Egypt and surrounding areas

The pyramid complex of King Zoser at Saqqâra, who reigned during the third dynasty

153

list of pharaohs and dynasties written by the priest Manetho in the third century BC.

The first and second dynasties of the Archaic period lasted until about 2650 BC under some twelve kings. Egypt already possessed many features of pharaonic culture. Great tombs made of sun-dried clay blocks were constructed for the kings. These preceded the use of pyramids for burial. During the first dynasty, the king was buried at Abydos, and during the second dynasty, at Saqqâra. Even after political unification, the pharaohs continued to bear the title "King of Upper and Lower Egypt." Around the royal burial sites were smaller tombs for the members of the court. All the graves contained burial gifts for the maintenance of the dead in the hereafter. Royal graves held many storage rooms filled with food and valuables far superior to those of his family members and servants.

The Old Kingdom: 2650–2150 BC

The first great period in Egyptian history lasted from the third to the sixth dynasty (from about 2650 to 2150 BC). The capital of the Old Kingdom was Memphis. The founder of its pyramid burial tradition was Zoser or Djoser, the second king of the third dynasty from about 2630 to 2611. He is noted for creating an administrative system for construction projects. His architect, Imhotep, constructed a tomb, like that of his predecessors, that was supposed to be a copy of his palace but much larger. He used stone blocks rather than the usual mud bricks. The result was a complex of buildings surrounded by a wall with niches cut in it to symbolize gates. Only one niche was the actual entrance. The buildings themselves, containing storage rooms and chapels, were massive but had only a symbolic function related to the celebration of the royal jubilee or sed. Through this ceremony, the power of the king was believed to be ritually renewed. At the center of the complex, a step pyramid, the actual tomb of Zoser, rises two hundred feet (61 meters) high, symbolizing the hill on which creation began. Smaller versions of it were built in earlier tombs.

During the fourth dynasty, the Memphite kingdom expanded its trade and mining interests. Pyramid construction reached its peak. Under its first king, Snefru (2575–2551), the first true pyramid was built at Dahshur. His son Cheops (or Khufu) (2551–2528) built the Great Pyramid at Giza. Cheops's son Reldjedef, pharaoh from about 2528 to 2520, introduced Re, the sun

Painted wooden figure of a female servant brewing beer, dating from the end of the Old Kingdom, about 2300 BC

Wooden statue of an official and his wife, dating from the fifth dynasty

154

The King and the Gods

The word *pharaoh* comes via Hebrew from the Egyptian word *per a'a* (Great House), a name for the royal palace and later for the king himself. The kingdoms of Egypt were theocratic. Pharaohs held absolute power and enjoyed divine status: They were seen to embody the creator of the world, spanning it in the guise of a great falcon. The pharoah was therefore often depicted as a falcon.

The Egyptian monarchy was based on concepts similar to those in many ancient monarchies: The monarch was believed to guarantee the fertility and the prosperity of society simply through his existence. He was considered to be in touch with invisible powers (gods or ancestors) with whom he could negotiate on behalf of his subjects. He was thus the appropriate person to make sacrifices to the gods and to converse with them, but since he could not be in every temple at the same time, priests carried out these tasks in his place. The awe-inspiring size of the pyramids, the royal burial sites, is explained in part by religious belief. Even though a new pharaoh reigned after the death of the old, the body of the old king had to be preserved and honored in order for the world to survive.

Inscriptions found in the pyramids of the fifth and sixth dynasties indicate that a pharaoh was not considered truly a god until after his death. After his death, the king was thought to become Osiris, King of the Dead. These texts introduce many other gods as well. The king had a special relationship with each of them. In the late Old Kingdom, the gods became increasingly important with respect to the king, especially Osiris, the god of the dead, and the sun god, Re. Their principal temples were to be found in the cities of Heliopolis and Abydos, respectively. Reldjedef, the son of Cheops, who reigned about 2528 to 2520 BC, first emphasized Re (or Ra, the solar ruler of the sky) in Egyptian religion, making it part of the proper title of the pharaoh. The king was called the "Son of Re" from then on. He was also called Horus, the falcon god, son of Osiris.

Limestone grave stele of King Djet (sometimes spelled Wadj), found in Abydos (first dynasty, around 2850 BC). Under the snake sign, which stands for the name *Djet*, is shown the facade of the king's palace or mortuary temple. The falcon figure above it symbolizes the deceased king himself and also part of the royal name.

Painted limestone statue of a scribe sitting, probably from the fifth dynasty. The Egyptian administration needed many skillful scribes, who held a privileged position in society.

the status of the pharaohs. This continued in the sixth dynasty.

Society under the Old Kingdom

The organization of the labor force required for the construction of these pyramids indicates the great power the king held over society. Thousands of workers were needed and they had to be supervised, fed, and sheltered during construction. The kings apparently used both their own private resources and money obtained from levying taxes. Frequent censuses were taken. Payment or work obligations were exacted but could sometimes be exempted. Individuals in charge of sacrificial ceremonies at temples and graves, for example, were protected under royal decrees.

Important officials were often relatives of the king. The *vizier* (or chief minister) was often his son. *Nomarchs,* the officials who governed *nomes* (provinces), were drawn from local families. Governors could also be given other assignments. During the sixth dynasty, around 2200 BC, Nomarch Harkhuf of Aswân was sent on an expedition to Nubia (now Sudan). Among the exotic items he returned with was a Pygmy, with whom the king was delighted. Other expeditions were sent to Punt (now Somalia), to the Sinai Peninsula, and to Byblos (modern Lebanon).

Deceased officials were interred in *mastabas,* rectangular stone graves surrounding the pyramids. Mastaba chapels were beautifully decorated with scenes from the daily life of the deceased.

Except for minor military expeditions like Snefru's campaigns in Nubia, Libya, and the Sinai, and the increased incursions of the fifth dynasty into Asia, Egypt had no conflicts with its neighbors under the Old Kingdom and no standing army. It was protected by its natural borders: the deserts in the west and east and the first cataract of the Nile in the south.

Great success in the Old Kingdom was not limited to the engineering and architecture of the pyramids. It also produced notable sculpture and painting and made significant advances in science and medicine, especially in anatomy, surgery, and antiseptics. Memphite astronomers excelled at navigation and created the first solar calendar with a year of 365 days.

god, into the religion. His brother Chephren (or Khafre) (2520–2494) succeeded him, building the second pyramid at Giza. Mycerinus (or Menkaure), who reigned about 2490 to 2472, built the third and smallest of the three main pyramids there.

The first use of "Pyramid Texts," carvings on the walls of pyramid chambers, dates from the last king of the next dynasty, Unas, reigning from about 2356 to 2323 BC. He was buried at Saqqâra. During this fifth dynasty, according to such inscriptions, bureaucracy grew, beginning to undermine

Wooden model of a ship and crew from the Middle Kingdom. Such models were included among the burial gifts. The deceased is shown on the left, dressed in a tightly fitting white robe.

The Middle Kingdom

From the Chaotic Decline of the Old Kingdom, a Classical Culture Emerges

By the sixth dynasty, the authority of the kings began to wane. Even his wife conspired against Pepy I, who ruled from 2289 to 2255 BC. The *vizier* (chief minister) of Pepy II is said to have held unusual authority over the kingdom during that king's reign (2246–2152 BC). As the Old Kingdom drew to a close, its pharaohs were increasingly undermined by powerful local *nomarchs* (governors) no longer periodically posted out of their *nomes* (or districts). They built autonomous bases of power, forming competing factions in the north and south.

There was a rapid turnover of kings, still nominally in charge in Memphis, at the end of the sixth dynasty and throughout the seventh and eighth. Later, Egyptian royal lists and the chronicle of the priest Manetho mention scores of kings whose combined reigns extended over 150 years. Modern scholars estimate it to be a twenty-year period. The short reigns explain the scarcity of pyramids and other monuments from this era. No king had time for major construction. The weakened bureaucracy was another factor; the system required for huge mortuary projects no longer existed. The pyramid of Pepy II and the surrounding tombs of his servants, many built of clay, show a marked decline in size and quality.

157

First Intermediate Period

The seventh dynasty marked the beginning of the First Intermediate period, characterized by the rule of new dynasties of noble families elsewhere in the country. With the eighth dynasty, the domination of the Memphis kings came to a close. This had an effect on both architecture and religion. The massive works of the past could no longer be built, and nomarchs could now adopt inscription details for their own tombs.

Times were difficult. From the inscriptions on their tombs, we see that nomarchs took responsibility for their subjects as central authority collapsed. There is mention of a famine, possibly caused by low water levels in the Nile. Drought forced large groups of desert dwellers to move to the Nile Valley.

In the north, nomarchs near Herakleopolis established the ninth and tenth dynasties between about 2134 and 2040 BC, spreading north to the delta and Memphis and south to Asyût (Lycopolis). Their best-known rulers are Menkaure and Akhthoes. The tomb of a lesser potentate of this era, Ankhtifi, was found further south in el Molalla.

The literature of the time reflects its pessimistic outlook. It describes general economic misery and social change, as illustrated by the following passage from *Ipuwer's Warnings:* "But now the noblemen are sad, and the poor are happy. Each city says: Let us expel the powerful among us. Look! The poor of the land have become rich; the possessor of things [is now] the one who has nothing."

The new power structure and the change in status of local rulers were consistent with this image. Nomarch alliances resulted in the formation of two large territories: Thebes in the south and Herakleopolis in the north, reflecting the ancient opposition between Upper and Lower Egypt.

The Middle Kingdom and the Rise of Thebes

In Upper Egypt, nomarchs established the eleventh dynasty in Thebes, the ancient city the Greeks also called *Diospolis* (heavenly city). These nomarchs expanded their power northward and southward, particularly through campaigns against neighboring Koptos. One, Mentuhotep II (2061–2010 BC), finally conquered the north sometime after 2047 BC, again uniting Egypt under a single king with Thebes as the capital.

Coffin of a mummy from the seventeenth dynasty (ca. 1575 BC), found in Thebes. The coffin was created from a tree trunk and richly decorated.

Funerary temples of Mentuhotep I (eleventh dynasty, ca. 2010 BC), Tuthmosis III (eighteenth dynasty, ca. 1425), and Hatshepsut (eighteenth dynasty, ca. 1458). These temples were carved from the cliffs west of the Nile at Deir el-Bahri, near Thebes.

This was the start of the Middle Kingdom, commonly dated to include all of the eleventh dynasty, 2040 to 1640 BC, from the reunification of Egypt by Mentuhotep II. He generally kept control over the rebellious nomarchs.

Until that time, Thebes had been relatively insignificant. Here, Mentu was worshiped as a god portrayed with a falcon's head, primarily associated with battle. Remains of Middle Kingdom temples dedicated to Mentu have been uncovered near modern Luxor. Other major deities were the fertility god, Min, from Koptos and the local god, Amon, who took over the properties of Min and the sun god, Re, becoming Amon-Re, god of fertility and father of the gods. The largely undamaged ruins of a temple to him can be seen today in Thebes at Karnak. The Old Testament called Thebes *No* (city) or *No-Amon* (city of Amon).

Many other great temples and monuments were erected in and around Thebes during this period. In the valley of Deir el-Bahri, on

Limestone *stele* (gravestone) of a high official from the Middle Kingdom, ca. 2000 BC

Bronze statuette of the god Anubis, keeper of cemeteries and god of mummifying

159

Replica
of an Egyptian
sailboat

the west bank of the Nile opposite Luxor, Mentuhotep built his own rock tomb with a separate mortuary temple. In part, this continued the tradition of the Old Kingdom pyramids, which also had temples connected to them, but his had no pyramid. The temple was dedicated not merely to the king himself, but to the gods, initially to Mentu and later to Amon-Re. Under it were the tombs of Mentuhotep's wives.

Elsewhere in Egypt, Mentuhotep erected other temples to the gods. Their reliefs show a resurgence of quality after the artistic decline of the First Intermediate period, brought on by the absence of a royal court.

King Amenemhet I (Ammenemes I)

Under Mentuhotep III, a major expedition, led by the vizier Amenemhet, was mounted to Wadi Hammammat in the eastern desert. Inscriptions on the site indicate that its purpose was to obtain *graywacke* (a dark gray stone) for the king's sarcophagus. It was probably this vizier who took the throne as King Amenemhet I after the death of

Mentuhotep III. The reason for his accession is not known, but Manetho starts a new dynasty, the twelfth, at this point.

That his ascent was unexpected is suggested by a propagandistic literary text of this period, *The Prophecy of Neferti*. King Snefru of the Old Kingdom receives ominous predictions from Neferti about Egypt's future, probably reflecting the chaotic First Interregnum. In her prophecy, a king named Ameni rises from the south to restore order by force. Portrayed as the savior of Egypt, the king is undoubtedly a reference to Ammenemes intended to minimize the significance of the previous dynasty. The story is a striking example of the way literature was used during the era to serve the purposes of the ruling king. He was depicted as more accessible, more human than the godlike pharaohs of the past.

Although he may have come to power through violence, Amenemhet's reign was peaceful. He revived the traditions of the Old Kingdom, diminishing the importance of Thebes and moving the court to the north again. He founded a new capital just south of Memphis. However, he still accorded Amon, god of Thebes, the ranking position in the hierarchy of gods. Close to the city, he built a pyramid for himself, an example subsequent kings would follow.

Amenemhet stressed the importance of national unity, insisting that the nomarchs recognize his authority while still permitting them to retain power. He reshaped Egypt's internal administration and had a new staff of scribes educated. He reinforced the borders, building a "kings wall" east of the Nile Delta to prevent the entrance of people from Sinai, and began construction of large fortresses along the Nile in Nubia. He kept the western desert people subdued by means of military expeditions.

To ensure smooth succession, Amenemhet ruled jointly with his son, Sesostris, during his final years. The king was assassinated in a court conspiracy while Sesostris was on a military expedition. Some of the circumstances surrounding Ammenemes's death are identical to those found in a literary text of the period, *The Story of Sinuhe*. The hero Sinuhe participated in a campaign led by the crown prince and was afraid that he would be involved in the court intrigue. He fled to Palestine and, after years of roaming, was finally requested to return to Egypt by the new king, Sesostris I, who had succeeded his father despite the conspiracy. In the *Lesson of Amenemhet,* the deceased king advises his son to trust no one: A king has no friends, he said, only heavy responsibility.

Middle Egyptian Literature

The texts of the Middle Kingdom provide considerable historical information; their exceptional style makes them absorbing works of literature, as well. Rather than exhibiting the archaic stiffness and elaborate praise of tomb inscriptions, they are lively and occasionally even critical of society. Some have the emphasis on practical details seen in works from the Old Kingdom.

Old Egyptian was the written form of the language used in the Predynastic period through the six dynasties of the Old Kingdom, from before 3000 to about 2200 BC. It was replaced during the Middle Kingdom by Middle Egyptian, the classical Egyptian of literature. Spoken Egyptian changed over time and became increasingly remote from classical grammar. Middle Egyptian, used from about 2200 to 1600, continued exclusively in written form until about 500.

The overriding tone of Middle Kingdom literature is disillusionment with established tradition, undoubtedly the result of the

Statue of King Ammenemes III, who reigned during the twelfth dynasty, about 1800 BC

161

Life in Ancient Egypt

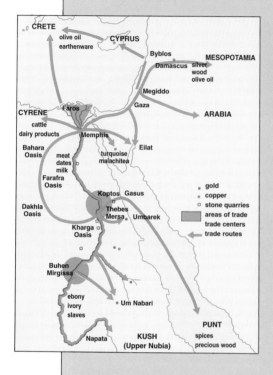

Economic Resources
and Trade Routes of Ancient
Egypt

The majority of the Egyptian people worked on the scant areas of fertile land renewed by the Nile. Their lives were dominated by its annual flooding, which determined the cycle of plowing, sowing, and harvesting. The major crops were wheat and barley, used for bread and beer and flax for linen. In the oases or irrigated areas, the major horticultural products included grapes, dates, and figs. Meat was supplied by cattle and poultry and, to a lesser extent, by pigs, goats, and desert animals. Fishing and hunting were important means of livelihood, as was the gathering of fruit and nuts.

The society was strictly regulated in a number of aspects, notable in the settlements established by the government for artisans, civil servants, and temple personnel. They were provided small houses and wages in kind, usually food rations. Slaves, often prisoners of war, were used in construction work on pyramids, temples, and palaces and kept by private individuals, as well.

According to the letters of Hekanakhte from the period of Mentuhotep II, there was ample opportunity for well-to-do Egyptians to acquire and expand private holdings. Hekanakhte, a funerary priest, owned several plots of land and leased more that were cultivated by his sons and servants. With the proceeds, he was able to support his extensive household. His relatives complained about the portions they were given, especially when he decided to take a second wife!

Farmers taking grain
to a silo. Wall painting from a
tomb of the eleventh dynasty,
about 2000 BC

Decorated limestone burial stele from the eleventh dynasty for Meru, an official, who is seated with his wife at a loaded offering table (ca. 2040 BC)

chaotic First Intermediate period. There are many works with a clearly political slant, like *The Prophecy of Neferti, The Lesson of Ammenemes,* and *Sinuhe,* all concerned with the royal house. Stories frequently contain a justification or glorification of the king's behavior. The idea of royal power as responsibility is a recurring theme.

Literary texts were written on papyrus, a kind of paper made by cutting out lengths of pith from papyrus reeds, crisscrossing and soaking them in layers in water, and pressing them flat with a piece of ivory or shell. (Our words *paper* and *papyrus* are based on the Egyptian word *pa per a'a,* "that which Pharaoh owns.") The dried rolls of papyrus were inscribed in ink with abbreviated versions of hieroglyphs.

Slaughtering of a cow; wall painting from an eleventh-dynasty tomb, ca. 2000 BC

The Greek word *hieroglyph* means "sacred carving," indicating the original use of this pictorial script on stone monuments. Hieroglyphics had two cursive or written developments. The first, hieratic ("priestly") script, was named by the Greeks for its original use in religious texts. It was widely used from this era to about 650 BC when the second one, demotic ("popular") script, began to replace it. Demotic writing was used until about AD 450. In both scripts, symbols represented ideas, and syllables had only consonants, no vowels. There were single letters and signs for words with more than one meaning. The Egyptians themselves believed that their script had been taught to them by Thoth, the god of science and writing, and called it "the words of the gods."

Death and the Hereafter

The disillusionment expressed in Middle Egyptian literature extended to belief in the hereafter: Harpists' songs called on the listeners to enjoy life on earth, because only decline awaited them after death. A pessimistic story illustrates this, a dialogue between a man and his soul or *ba*. The man is tired of life and considering suicide. His ba, preferring earthly life, threatens to leave him if he goes through with it. This was in striking contrast to the earlier Egyptian belief in life after death as a happier reflection of life on earth.

The images of life after death that have survived from the Old Kingdom mainly involved the pharaoh. After his death, he was said to become a god, with his living and dead subjects as dependents. This view changed during the First Intermediate period. The deceased Egyptian was no longer purely dependent on his king; he himself could gain divine state by becoming one with Osiris, the god of death. His body was embalmed, swathed in linen, and buried in a rectangular wooden coffin or sarcophagus. The insides of these coffins were decorated with magic sayings, the "sarcophagus texts," intended to help the deceased reach the hereafter safely by providing answers to difficult questions he would be asked. This knowledge in addition to his impeccable behavior was of major importance in obtaining life after death.

For his future life, the deceased was given food and representative objects intended to serve him, including wooden figurines of servants, models of entire workshops, ships and crews, and armies. *Ushebtis* or *shawabtis* accompanied the deceased, figures portraying him performing tasks he might be assigned in the hereafter. Ushebtis and shawabtis allude both to their function,

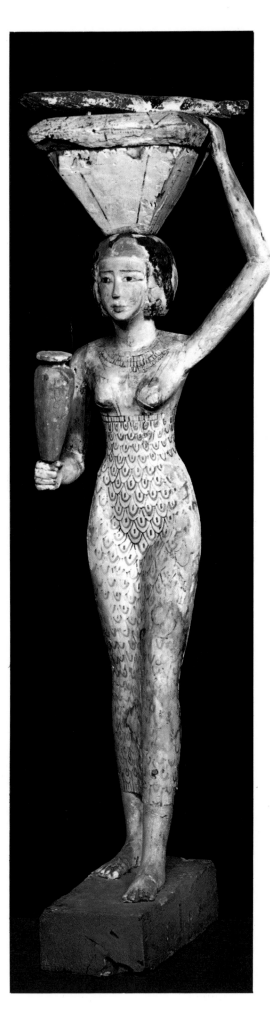

Wooden statue of a woman servant carrying funeral offerings, dating from ca. 2250 BC

Figurine depicting Thoth, the god of writing

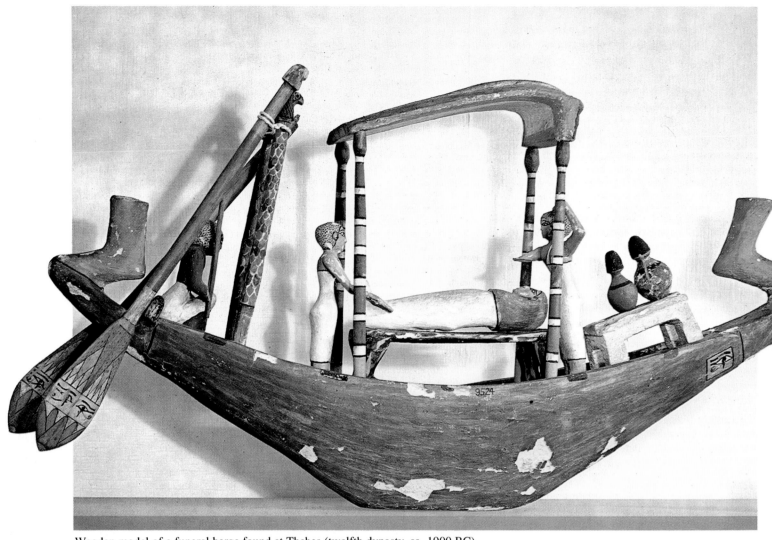

Wooden model of a funeral barge found at Thebes (twelfth dynasty, ca. 1900 BC)

answering to the gods, and to the substance they were initially made of; *usheb* means "answer" and *shawab* is persea wood.

Although provided with their own burial equipment, the dead were expected to require additional food. They remained dependent on the king. He had to appease the gods so they would receive and feed his subjects. The *steles* (tombstones), which expressed the deceased's wish to continue to receive food, always start with the words "an offering given by the king."

The offerings were not only symbolic; the surviving next of kin made actual food offerings to deceased relatives, usually on holy days. The rich could also hire special priests for this purpose, who were often connected

King Sesostris III
makes an offering to Mentu.
Temple relief from
Medamud near Luxor,
about 1850 BC

166

to the local temple. The tomb of the provincial administrator Djefai-Hapi near Asyut, from the twelfth dynasty, contains wall inscriptions listing a number of contracts he had made with priests prior to his death committing them to make offerings at his burial chapel. Their reward consisted of the offerings themselves. After his death, he, like the gods, could consume the offerings only in spirit. The offered bread, beer, and meat remained for the priests after the ritual, a common practice.

The Height of the Middle Kingdom

The twelfth dynasty lasted from 1991 to 1783 BC. The years can be calculated exactly, thanks to the astronomical observations of the Egyptians during this period. For two centuries, Egypt experienced major political and economic growth. The policies of Ammenemes I were adopted by his successors, each of whom ruled jointly with their respective crown princes for the last few years of their reigns.

Sesostris I, son of Ammenemes I, reigned from 1962 to 1926 BC, expanding the range of Egypt's interests. He built forts in Nubia, south of Egypt, established commercial ties with Palestine and Syria, and fought Libyans in the west. His territorial expansion was fueled by economic interests, particularly in Nubia; the area contained gold deposits. (The name *Nubia* is derived from *nub*, the Egyptian word for gold). Valuable materials were sought elsewhere, as well: In the eastern desert, numerous inscriptions bear testimony to large-scale expeditions involving thousands of people and beasts of burden to mine high-grade stone for the construction of monuments.

Within Egypt itself, arable land was perhaps the most valuable resource. Sesostris II, who ruled from 1897 to 1878 BC, was noted for reclaiming land in El Faiyûm (the Faiyûm oasis) to the west of the Nile Valley. Recent archaeologists have found the remains of the wooden floodgates he built.

Sesostris III, in power from 1878 to 1843 BC, had a passageway created through the first rocky cataract of the Nile, allowing access past it for the first time. This necessitated a defensive watch and the construction of large fortresses on the heights above the Nile. Nubians and Kushites were not allowed past these fortresses unless they intended to trade. Sesostris III formed a standing army to campaign against the Nubians and built new forts on the southern frontier. He divided the administration into four powerful geographic units, each controlled by an official under the vizier. He ended the threat to his power and the independence of the nomarchs, driving

Statue of King Ammenemes III, who reigned around 1800 BC

them and their families from position. From then on, the court, located in Memphis since the time of Ammenemes I, was represented throughout Egypt by a tight system of royal supervisors. A political reformer, Sesostris was also a successful conqueror, establishing Semna, a little south of the second cataract, as the newest border outpost. His troops penetrated far into Palestine, reaching the cities of Jerusalem and Sichem.

His successor, Amenemhet III (1844-1797 BC), continued those policies, particularly land reform.

167

Second Intermediate Period: The Hyksos

During the thirteenth dynasty of the Theban kings, Egypt had some seventy pharaohs in roughly 140 years. Again, their overall power weakened, but this time the decline was not caused by domestic potentates, although the rival fourteenth dynasty had gained the delta. The threat came from the northeast, the scene of Egyptian military successes under Sesostris III.

In the Near East, a tribal migration had been going on for some time, a ripple effect perhaps caused, in part, by the arrival of new peoples from the Caucasus in western Asia. The new arrivals drove out many of the Semitic people living in coastal Phoenicia, Levant, and the Sinai Peninsula, sending them into Egypt. Egyptian texts as early as the twelfth dynasty, mention people, referred to as "Asiatics," with Semitic names. Several pharaohs of the thirteenth dynasty bore non-Egyptian names like Chenger and Aya, indicating foreign origin.

Concurrent with this assimilation of foreigners into Egyptian society, non-Egyptian kingdoms from western Asia arose in the delta. The Egyptians called these new rulers *Hekau-chasut* (desert kings). This word appears in the writings of historians from the Greek period as "Hyksos." They established a dynasty (called the fifteenth) and a capital at Avaris in the eastern delta, dominating central and northern Egypt and rivaling the sixteenth dynasty in the same territory.

The time of decline following the twelfth dynasty and the rule of the Hyksos is called the Second Intermediate period. It lasted 250 years. The many pharaohs who ruled in quick succession (and often simultaneously) were divided by Manetho into three dynasties, the fourteenth through the sixteenth.

It is possible to relate this period in Egyptian history with the time of the patriarchs of the Bible. Jacob, who, according to the book of Genesis, settled in Egypt, and his son Joseph, who became the viceroy of the pharaoh, could very well have been referred to by the Egyptians as Asiatics or Hyksos, but this is by no means certain.

The Egyptian kings of the seventeenth Theban dynasty tried to maintain their power, ruling over the territory between Elephantine and Abydos. They were squeezed between two new powers, the Hyksos in the north and the kingdom of Kush in the south. Unlike the First Intermediate period, this period was marked not by internal administrative or economic crisis, but by the rise of these foreign rulers on the borders. There was no cultural decline. The Hyksos introduced new ideas and technology that greatly influenced pharaonic culture. Canaanite gods like Baal and Astarte appeared among the new Egyptian decorative motifs. A major military innovation, the horse-drawn chariot, made other methods of warfare obsolete.

Officials measuring a wheat field and recording the yield from the wheat harvest. Mural in Menna's tomb at Thebes, New Kingdom (eighteenth dynasty, ca. 1400 BC)

A column of hieratic text from the Ebers Papyrus, one of the world's oldest medical texts, written during the New Kingdom (eighteenth dynasty, ca. 1520 BC)

Votive stele of painted limestone, depicting two workmen paying tribute to Pharaoh Amenhotep I (1525-1504 BC), eighteenth dynasty

The Mighty Empire of Egypt

When the Hyksos Were Expelled, the Country Became a Military Superpower

While the Asiatics invading the Nile Delta established their own kingdoms, the native kings withdrew to Upper Egypt. Monuments to the last kings of the thirteenth dynasty have been found only there. During the seventeenth dynasty (1640-1550 BC), the Theban kings reigned over the territory between Elephantine and Abydos. The Hyksos rulers governed from Avaris in the eastern delta, probably located on the site of modern Tell el-Dab'a. Excavations in this area have revealed buildings and utensils similar to those made earlier in Syria and Palestine. Many objects appear to have been

Alabaster sphinx of
a pharaoh of the eighteenth
or nineteenth dynasty
in Memphis

Squatting statue
in pink quartzite portraying
a land surveyor of the
eighteenth dynasty

imported from there. A wealth of pottery in both Cypriot Minoan and Mycenaean styles has also been found, evidence of trade.

The Hyksos may also have been in Egypt at this time. The remains of temples found there, at Tell el-Dab'a, show the same design as others excavated in Israel and Syria. These were dedicated to, among other gods, Baal, a counterpart of Seth, the Egyptian god of aggression and chaos.

King Seqenenre of the seventeenth dynasty launched a war against the Hyksos from Thebes. He probably died in battle; his mummy shows fatal injuries. His son Kamose (reigned 1555-1550 BC) continued the conquest of the north. Kamose recounts his successful expedition on a stele now in the Museum of Luxor. Thebes became such a threat to Apophis, the king of the Hyksos, that he tried to form an alliance with the king of Kush, far to the south, to force the Egyptians to fight on two fronts at once. However, the Hyksos messenger, sent south through the oasis of the western desert to make the proposal to the Kushites, was taken

Limestone relief representing Queen Tiy, the wife of Amenhotep III (ca. 1375 BC)

Limestone figurine of Pharaoh Amenhotep I (1525-1504 BC, eighteenth dynasty)

prisoner by Kamose's soldiers. The alliance may never have materialized. Kamose drove the Hyksos back to the walls of Avaris but could not take the city. This fell to his successor, King Ahmose I.

The New Kingdom: 1550-1070 BC

The expulsion of the Hyksos and the reunification of Egypt by Ahmose I marked the beginning of Egypt's third great period, the New Kingdom. Later historians considered Ahmose as the founder of a new dynasty, the eighteenth (1550-1307 BC), which included such famous rulers as the only woman pharaoh, Hatshepsut; Thutmose III; Akhenaton; and Tutankhamen. This age is particularly noted for the military feats and the religious efforts of its pharaohs and for its art, which became less rigid, perhaps due to the influence of eastern and Aegean civilizations.

171

Mural of a feast
from a Theban tomb of
the New Kingdom.
The guests are served
by scantily clad
servant girls.

The Eighteenth Dynasty Kings

Ahmose I did not confine his military enterprises merely to ousting the Hyksos. He pursued them into Palestine, establishing the basis for Egyptian presence in western Asia, of vital importance because of the copper mines located there. In the south, he subjugated the kingdom of Kush. He made good use of his army, paying it well to keep the still-powerful nomarchs at bay. He revived the administration and the programs of the Middle Kingdom, including land reclamation begun by Sesostris II at El Faiyûm.

His attention was also needed at home. An inscription tells how Ahmose, who had just passed through Thebes, was forced to return because of a sudden storm. It was the god Amon showing his dissatisfaction with his residence, which had hardly been changed since the twelfth century. In Thebes, once again the empire's capital, he started to restore and enlarge the temples of Amon.

Amon became the principal deity of the dynasty. The king, considered the son of Amon, accorded him highest rank. The queen was also included in this concept, considered no longer just the king's wife, but also Amon's. In a mystical marriage, she conceived a son by Amon, who was the god regarded as the rightful heir to the throne, a child of both Amon and the king. This reinforced continuation of the dynasty on a religious level.

Ahmose's son and successor, Amenhotep I (1525-1504 BC), reigned with him as co-regent for five years before taking full authority in 1525 BC. He introduced the office of "King's Son of Kush" to govern the recently colonized region. Ruling until 1504, Amenhotep I further expanded Egypt's borders in Nubia and the Levant.

Valley of the Kings

As Thebes became the center of the empire, it was also made the place where its kings were buried. Prior to the New Kingdom, pharaohs had often been buried in the pyramids. As early as the seventeenth dynasty, they were interred in tombs in the mountains on the western shore of the Nile. These typically had a sacrificial chapel with a miniature pyramid called a *pyramidion*. In the tomb chamber, hewn from rock, the king was laid in a wooden mummy case, shaped like a man. Amenhotep deviated from the custom, building his temple nearer the riverbank. Although his tomb has not been located with certainty, he was the first king to hide his burial place, making it separate from his mortuary temple. This initiated a new custom, but the kings after him had their tombs built in Thebes's Valley of the Kings. The valley is hidden by high cliffs and can be approached only through a narrow passage. The move may have been an attempt to avoid the grave plundering already prevalent. Tuthmose I (1504-1492 BC), who followed Amenhotep I, was the first of many pharaohs to be buried there. Like the other tombs, it was concealed after it was closed.

Sixty-two tombs have been found at this burial site, most with several rooms carved into solid rock. The first, belonging to Seti I, was discovered empty in AD 1817 by an Italian, G. B. Belzoni. Seti's body was found, together with the reburied mummies of thirty-nine other pharaohs, in a single vault in 1881. Their wives, except for Hatshepsut, queen of Tuthmose II and a ruler herself, are buried outside the valley, a few miles (five kilometers) away.

Embalming, the preservation of bodies after death, seems to have been practiced by the Egyptians over the course of thirty centuries. Bodies of animals (probably sacred animals, or possibly pets), as well as humans, have been excavated. Evidently considered a way to allow the body to stay united with the soul after death, it is generally regarded as a religious custom. Mummies were made by the following procedures: removing the brain and internal organs; dehydrating the body with natron (carbonate and salts) for forty days; packing the cavity with fragrant herbs and sawdust; treating with resin; and wrapping.

Hatshepsut and Tuthmose III

Tuthmose II (1492-1479 BC), son of a minor

Squatting red granite statue of Pharaoh Amenhotep II, about 1427-1401 BC

Mural depicting dancers during a feast, New Kingdom

wife of Tuthmose I, succeeded his father. He married the princess Hatshepsut to improve his royal claim. When he died around 1479 BC, his successor, Tuthmose III, was still a child. He nevertheless ascended the throne, ruling the country nominally, while his stepmother, Hatshepsut supervised its affairs as regent. Six years later, she claimed to see a statue of Amon move toward her during a festal procession. Considering herself selected by the god, Hatshepsut had herself proclaimed king. A similar selection had been claimed earlier by Tuthmose II, who was not the only candidate for succession to the throne.

According to tradition, Hatshepsut could not succeed to the throne as a woman; Tuthmose and Hatshepsut reigned jointly. Each of their names is enclosed in a *cartouche*, the oval frame in which royal names were written. Hatshepsut, however, played a more prominent role. Conveying an important message, she built her own monuments, including obelisks in Karnak and her funerary temple in Deir el-Bahri. In the inscrip-

Limestone statue
of the god Amon, who
played a major role
as Egypt's official god during
the New Kingdom

tions on them, Hatshepsut claimed it was only her rule that put an end to the chaos of the Hyksos era. Her revival of Old and Middle Kingdom traditions reinforced the return of stability. Usually portrayed as a man to comply with the traditional conception of the ruler, she was frequently depicted as an army commander, but there are no records of wars during her reign. She did organize expeditions abroad, including a voyage to the African country of Punt (Somalia). Pictures of the trip are found in her funerary temple: the misshapen wife of a local king; houses built on stilts; returning ships laden with incense, myrrh, monkeys, and exotic objects.

This changed drastically when Thutmose III became the sole monarch after Hatshepsut's death in 1458 BC. Perhaps furious because his stepmother had kept him in the background, late in his reign he had her name and image obliterated from all monuments, even the graves of her courtiers.

Tuthmose launched great wars of con-

Storage chest for
cosmetics and perfumes
from the eighteenth
dynasty, ca. 1400 BC

quest, retaking the entire Syro-Palestinian area. During his reign, the Egyptian kingdom reached its widest expanse, even reaching the Euphrates River in northern Mesopotamia. His expeditions are portrayed on the temple walls of Karnak.

The entire Near East was in turmoil at this time. The migrations that had brought the Hyksos to Egypt also fostered the development of new kingdoms in northern Mesopotamia, those of the Hurrians. The largest of these was Mitanni. Tuthmose tried but could not defeat it. Finally he formed an alliance. It was later reinforced through several generations of marriage. Tuthmose and his successors, Amenhotep II, Tuthmose IV, and Amenhotep III, all took Mitanni princesses as brides. Tuthmose also expanded Egypt to the south, establishing a new border beyond Napata in what had been Kush territory.

Amenhotep II, who reigned from 1427 to 1401 BC, and Tuthmose IV, reigning from 1401 to 1391, used both military and diplomatic means to maintain power. For some time a balance of power would exist among these kingdoms, but other powers were on the rise: the Assyrians and the Hittites.

Social Organization of the New Kingdom

As both a political and a religious leader, the pharaoh remained aloof from the rest of society. His reputed contact with the gods was said to guarantee the country's prosperity. Seen as the guardian of all mankind, as legislator and military commander, he maintained order on Earth and throughout the universe. As long as that order–*Ma'at* in Egyptian–was not disrupted, the world would continue to exist. The pharaoh, following consultation with his officials, would issue laws and formulate decrees. In practice, much of the responsibility for legislation must have rested on his highest administrators, especially the vizier. In the tomb of Rekhmire, who was vizier under Hatshepsut and Thutmose III, an extensive job description of that office has been preserved. It is referred to as the "bitter task." The long enumeration of his duties shows that the vizier was responsible for maintaining order in the royal court and for the control of taxation, the royal treasuries, and the grain silos. He was also required to supervise the lower administrators and punish them for infractions.

The majority of the population worked in agriculture, the basis of the Egyptian economy. Other professions, however, developed. Administrators, priests, artisans, and especially army officers became more influential. Regular military campaigns made it necessary to keep large numbers of soldiers on

Granite statue of the god Amon with the Pharaoh Tutankhamen before him, 1333-1323 BC

175

alert—and to pay for their services. Within the army, there were different ranks and positions; the major distinction was between the infantrymen and the charioteers. The commander in chief was the pharaoh. His princes were taught to manage horses and weapons at an early age.

Gods and Temples

The king was obliged to appease the gods regularly by offering sacrifices and by build-

Mural from Tutankhamen's tomb in the Valley of the Kings at Thebes, portraying the deceased pharaoh as Osiris, ca. 1323 BC

ing and expanding their temples. The Egyptian temple, which we know in its classical form only from the New Kingdom, was designed to allow for continuous expansion. Its core was the sanctum, where the image of the god resided and was cared for by the priests. They acted as representatives of the king. Only the highest priests were allowed to enter this part of the temple, beyond the colonnades and open courtyards. Major temples, like those at Karnak and Luxor, could be enlarged by adding new halls or courts to the existing ones, all forming a straight line from the sanctum to the *pylon* (or temple gate).

The priests serving in the temple were sons of important families. Administrators and laborers also worked in them. Sub-

stantial resources were required to make the requisite religious sacrifices, feed the employees, and maintain the sanctuary itself. The pharaoh supplied those resources in the form of agricultural fields, grassland, and cattle. In addition to this ordinary income, the temple received regular gifts of valuable objects that the king brought from his campaigns or trading expeditions. The wars of Thutmose III, for example, contributed hundreds of pounds of gold and silver to the temple of Amon.

The priesthood was, for the most part, an honorary position that could be taken on by officials, in addition to their administrative tasks, as a source of extra income. Offices and their salaries were usually passed on from father to son. The king had to pay serious attention to the interests of these families of priests and officials. Through his careful

The Religion of Aton

The sun god, Re (or Ra), held an important place in the traditional polytheistic religion of Egypt, but as one of many gods. Murals in

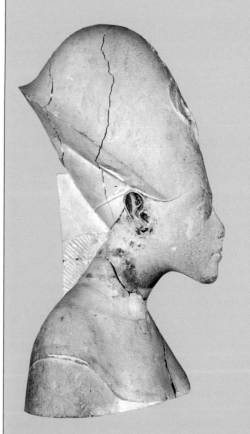

Limestone bust of Akhenaton from Tel el Amarna, about 1350 BC

176

attendance to temples, he at once placated the gods and maintained a loyal staff of servants throughout the country.

The Amarna Period

During the rule of Amenhotep III (1391-1353 BC), Egypt reached the peak of its power and development. Its wealth rested on agricultural production and the gold mined in Nubia. Egypt was considered an inexhaustible source of this precious metal. Gold was freely used to reinforce treaties with foreign kings. International trade prospered, as well, over this period.

It was an era of great architectural works. The remains of temples built by Amenhotep III are found primarily in Thebes and Nubia. On the western bank of the Nile, near Luxor, he built both an enormous funerary temple, where the Colossi of Memnon can still be seen, and a new palace facing a large artificial lake. The Colossus or great statue represents Memnon, who was, according to Greek mythology, the king of Ethiopia killed by the hero Achilles in the Trojan War. To assuage the grief of his mother, Eos, the goddess of dawn, the paramount god Zeus made him immortal.

Amenhotep III relied on negotiation in his foreign policy, and his long reign was noted for its peace as well as its accomplishments in art and architecture. Some of his diplo-

the royal tombs depict his journey through the underworld with the deceased pharaoh.

Pharaoh Amenhotep IV (reigning 1353-1335 BC) insisted that Re be worshiped as unique and under a different name, Aton (or Aten). Instituting monotheism in Egypt, he changed his own name to Akhenaton (Servant of Aton) and founded a new capital, Akhetaton (Aton's Horizon). Because Aton was visible in the sky, the temples in Akhetaton had no roofs or statues.

Aton was portrayed as the disk of the sun, a glowing circle devoid of all human features, a symbol taken from earlier depictions of Re. Images from Akhenaton's time show the disk with long rays ending in hands holding the ankh, the symbol of life. Akhenaton bestowed royal status on the god by writing his name in cartouches, pictorial oval frames reserved for the names of royalty.

matic correspondence has been preserved on the 400 clay tablets called the Amarna Letters.

These tablets were found by a peasant in the city Tel el Amarna, site of the ancient Egyptian city Akhetaton on the Nile River, in AD 1887. Inscribed in Akkadian cuneiform, they constitute part of the correspondence of Amenhotep III and his son and successor Amenhotep IV with the governors of Palestine and Syria and the kings of Babylonia, Assyria, and Mitanni. The letters provide significant information about the Amarna period.

Under Amenhotep IV (Akhenaton), who reigned from 1353 to 1335 BC, the country experienced a major religious reformation. Opposing the power of the Amon priests, this pharaoh made the sun god Re (or Ra-Harakhte from Heliopolis) the sole god in Egyptian religion. This deity already occupied an important place in the hierarchy of gods. While it was not unusual for one god to

This mural, found in the temple of Tuthmosis III, depicts Hathor, the Egyptian cow-goddess, giving milk to the pharaoh.

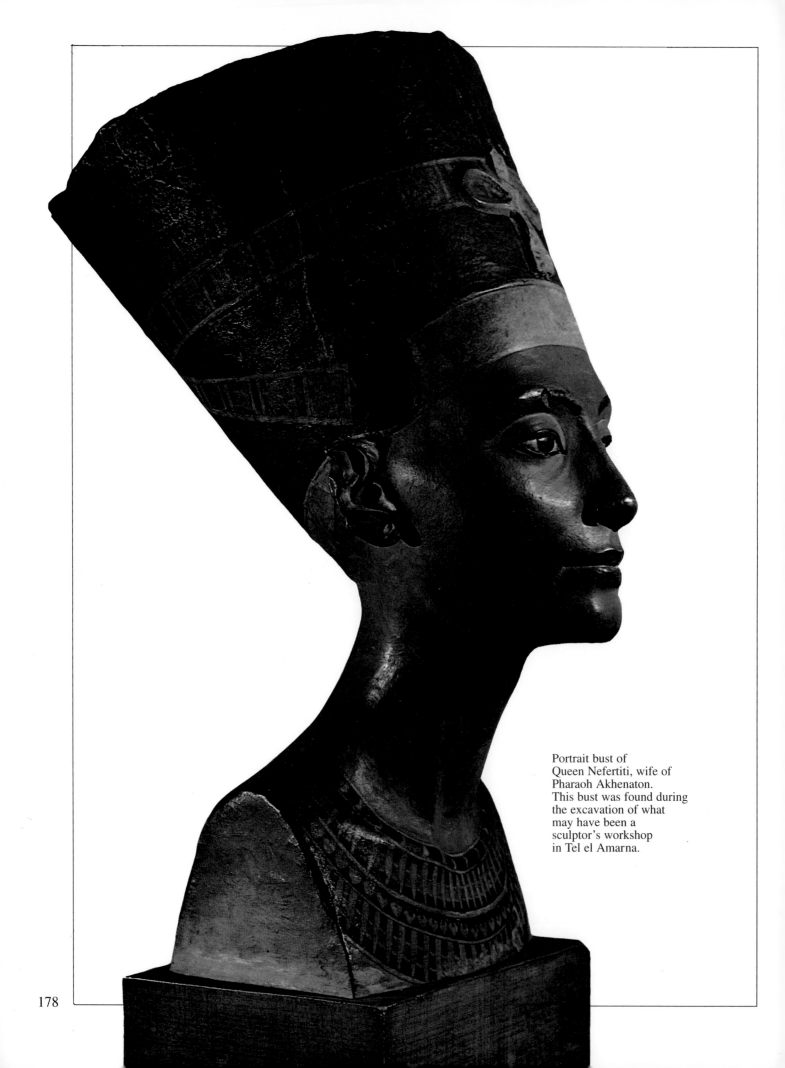

Portrait bust of
Queen Nefertiti, wife of
Pharaoh Akhenaton.
This bust was found during
the excavation of what
may have been a
sculptor's workshop
in Tel el Amarna.

178

be considered paramount, Amenhotep IV proceeded to deny the existence of any other divinities, instituting monotheism in Egypt. He demanded that the god be worshiped under a different name, Aton (or Aten), the disk of the sun. He changed his own name to Akhenaton ("Servant of Aton") and, as the son of Aton, he announced he was the only prophet of the new religion. This major change was marked by the celebration of the *sed* (or royal jubilee) the fourth year after Akhenaton's accession, although traditionally it did not take place until the thirtieth year of a pharaoh's reign. He had a special temple built for Aton in Karnak.

Akhenaton then left Thebes and founded a new capital, *Akhetaton* (Aton's Horizon), to honor Aton. He found it near today's Tel el Amarna in central Egypt. The *steles* (monuments) marking the city limits date from his sixth year. The new city became the location of a new royal court. Except for a few individuals, Akhenaton's court consisted entirely of new people. He obviously did not want anything to do with the old officials and priests. He even removed the images and names of all the gods but Re from monuments throughout Egypt. Constructed between 1348 and 1334 BC, the new city

Ruins of the great temple of Amon in Karnak, dating mainly from the New Kingdom

Relief on a column in the temple of Queen Hatshepsut (1473-1458 BC, eighteenth dynasty) in Deir el-Bahri, representing the queen and the god Amon

179

served as the country's capital until Akhenaton's death.

The change in religion was accompanied by other changes. The art of this age was more realistic in its portrayals, especially of the human figure. The representations of Akhenaton himself, his queen Nefertiti, and their daughters are almost caricatures. They are probably exaggerations of the king's actual physical features, including a gourd-shaped head, a narrow face with pulpy lips and a knobby chin, a potbelly, wide hips, and matchstick legs. Not all the images show these distortions; the fabulous bust of Nefertiti from Amarna is regarded as one of the most beautiful sculptures ever made.

About 1380 BC, Egyptian emerged as the new literary standard. It would be used for business and some priestly documents until about 700. Classic Middle Egyptian continued to be used in religious texts.

The Armarna Letters show that Akhenaton maintained contacts with other states through correspondence and the exchange of gifts, but it is clear that he neglected to take military action when Egypt began to lose its influence in the Syro-Palestinian region. He must have caused domestic tension, as well, by his dismissal of many officials and his neglect of the traditional temples and their priests.

King Smenkhkare, who reigned jointly with Akhenaton during his final years, abandoning the religious reformation, began to build temples again in Thebes. Akhenaton's son-in-law and successor, Tutankhamen, returned the capital to Thebes and started to repair the temples in the entire country. Again the historical change was expressed in a change of name: Tutankhamen was initially called Tutankhaten. His wife Ankhesenaten, a daughter of Akhenaton, changed her name to Ankhesenamen.

The eighteenth dynasty ended with Horemheb, who reigned from 1319 to 1307 BC. This formally ended the Amarna period. Akhenaton left such a bad impression that not only he, but his immediate successors as well, were omitted from the official royal lists. His name is not listed in Manetho's work. Only once, in a later reference, Akhenaton is mentioned as the "Enemy from Akhetaton."

Tutankhamen died young and was buried in a small, exquisitely decorated tomb in the Valley of the Kings. Probably the subsequent erasure of the Amarna period from Egyptian memory caused this tomb to be forgotten. It escaped the plundering that afflicted all the other royal graves, and was discovered practically untouched by the British archaeologists Howard Carter and Lord Carnarvon in AD 1922. Like the other tombs, its walls were covered with carved and painted hieroglyphics and representational scenes. Apparently robbed twice, it still held more than 5,000 items.

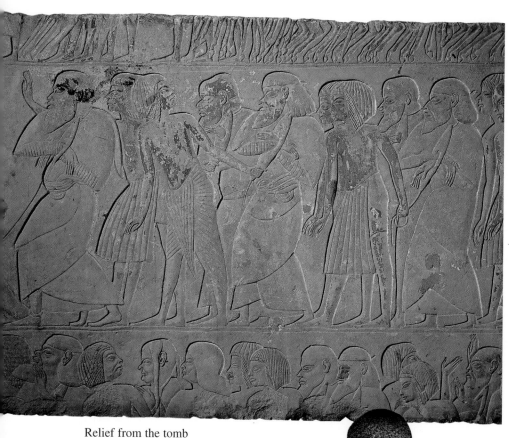

Relief from the tomb of Horemheb, a successful general and successor of Tutankhamen. This relief is part of a scene in which Horemheb is being honored as a conqueror. Egyptian soldiers are leading foreign prisoners.

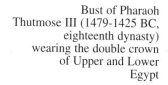

Bust of Pharaoh Thutmose III (1479-1425 BC, eighteenth dynasty) wearing the double crown of Upper and Lower Egypt

Part of the throne of Pharaoh Tutankhamen, made of gold and inlaid with glass and semiprecious stones. The throne formed part of the inventory of the pharaoh's grave, which was discovered and excavated in AD 1922.

The Fall of the New Kingdom

After the Ramesside Kings, the Egyptian Pharaohs Yielded to Foreign Domination

Tutankhamen succeeded his father-in-law, Akhenaton, in 1333 BC as pharaoh at about the age of nine. During his brief reign, he restored the traditional worship of Amon, abandoned by Akhenaton in favor of monotheism, and reestablished Thebes as the Egyptian capital. Not an important king in his lifetime, he is famous in death for his tomb, discovered in AD 1922. When he died at age eighteen in 1323 BC, Tutankhamen left a mourning widow — Ankhesenamen — and a throne, at once the stake in a power struggle. In the absence of a male heir, the successor was bound to be a high-ranking official. Two possible candidates were General Horemheb and Aya, an old official who had already served Akhenaton in Akhetaton. Rather than accepting either as her husband and the new pharaoh, Ankhesenamen wrote to Suppiluliuma, the Hittite king, asking for one of his sons to ascend the Egyptian throne. Suppiluliuma apparently had misgivings, but finally sent his son Zannanza, who was assassinated en route. This may have been by order of Aya, who took the throne and sent General Horemheb north against attacking Hittites.

The old king only lived another four years. Horemheb came to power in 1319 BC. A long decree dealing with administrative corruption attests to his efforts to restore order. Knowledge of his earlier career comes from the decoration of his tomb in Saqqâra, built while he served as a general to Tutankhamen. Its reliefs show Horemheb returning from a campaign in Syria to the rewards of the royal couple. The tomb would remain empty. As pharaoh, Horemheb had a more impressive one hewn for himself in the Valley of the Kings near Thebes. Horemheb, usually regarded as the last pharaoh of the eighteenth dynasty, died in 1307.

The Ramesside Kings (1307–1070 BC)

Horemheb's successor, General Parammessu, was also a soldier, taking the throne as Ramses I. Most of the kings in the nineteenth and twentieth dynasties took the same name. Ramses I only reigned from 1307 to 1306 BC, sharing power in his last year with his son, Seti I, who succeeded him.

Seti I

Under the successors of Ramses I, the large Egyptian Empire was able to hold its own, though not without violent battles. Seti I took

Statue
of Ramses II,
about
1250 BC

The Amarna Letters

After being inhabited for a mere ten years, Akhenaton's capital, Akhetaton, was abandoned. During the hasty departure, much was left behind, including the archive of the royal correspondence office. This archive, found in AD 1887, contains some 400 clay tablets written in Babylonian cuneiform. Babylonian was the predominant international language in the Near East during this era, the fourteenth century BC. The tablets are correspondence between the pharaohs Amenhotep III and Akhenaton and foreign rulers. These included the kings of Babylon, Mitanni, and the Hittites, who regarded the pharaoh their equal and addressed him as "my brother," and the rulers of city-states in the Syro-Palestinian region, who adopted a much more deferential tone. These small princes were unpredictable factors in the political power game because they would ally themselves first with one major power, then with another.

The letters clearly show how the older states were being exposed to new threats. These included the great Hittite Empire, one of the earliest civilizations in Asia Minor (modern Turkey), which continued to expand, and the roaming Chabiru tribes, who may have been the Hebrews of the Bible. There are letters describing how a former vassal of Egypt, Abdi-Ashirta of Amurru, formed an alliance with the Chabiru and later with the Hittites. King Rib-Addi of Byblos,

on the other hand, remained loyal to the pharaoh and repeatedly wrote that the Egyptian king must send troops quickly, to prevent Abdi-Ashirta and other kings from joining forces against Egypt.

In addition to the political information they contain, the letters are valuable for their language. The Canaanite writers did not use pure Babylonian, but a mixture of Babylonian and their own language. To a great extent, the suffixes of verbs resemble those of the much later Hebrew of the Bible. The Amarna Letters are, therefore, also important in describing the evolution of this language.

Fresco from the palace of Pharaoh Akhenaton in Tel el Amarna showing a duck flying from a stand of papyrus (1353-1335 BC, eighteenth dynasty)

Egyptian limestone statuette of pharaoh Akhenaton and his wife Nefertiti, dating from the Amarna period (1365-1349).The art of this period differed greatly from the traditional Egyptian art. The proportions of the human body are depicted in a more natural way, e.g. the legs are shorter, and the torso and neck are longer. After the Amarna period, however, the classical Egyptian art took over again.

A priest. Detail on a papyrus from the Book of the Dead

Breastplate of Ramses II found in the Serapeum near Memphis. The decorative piece is made of gold and inlaid with glass and semiprecious stones.

full control from 1306 to 1290 BC, campaigning to recover parts of Syria Egypt had lost, conquering Palestine, and battling the Hittites and tribes from the Libyan desert.

Seti began construction on the great hall of the temple to Amon at Karnak, which would be completed by his successor, Ramses II. In the ancient city of Abydos, he began a magnificent temple of white limestone, decorated with delicately painted reliefs, beautifully preserved to this day. Following the tradition practiced at the royal tombs in Thebes, he had the temple dedicated to himself as well

as Osiris, the patron god of the city. Seti's tomb was found in 1817 in the Valley of the Kings near Thebes. His mummy was not found until 1881 at Deir el-Bahri.

Seti's building projects were not limited to the temples. He built a new palace in Memphis, which had again become the seat of government, and another one in the eastern Nile Delta near the ancient Hyksos city of Avaris. The pharaoh was probably a native of this region. His son, Ramses II, succeeded him, reigning for some sixty-seven years.

Ramses II (1290–1224 BC)

It is probably after Ramses II, rather than Ramses I, that the next nine pharaohs took their name. He continued Seti's attempt to regain control in parts of Africa and western Asia held by Egypt in previous centuries. He annexed the territory of the once-rebellious Amorites, but the northern border, which continued to be threatened by the Hittites, was his prime source of concern. The city of Qadesh had fallen into Hittite hands, and Ramses had to act quickly to retain the Egyptian territory in its vicinity. The Hittite king, Muwatallis, turned out to be a formidable opponent.

Granite triad (representation of three persons) portraying Pharaoh Ramses II (1290-1224 BC, nineteenth dynasty) seated between the god Amon and the goddess Mut

185

The battle at Qadesh in 1285 BC was made famous by the hieroglyphic descriptions and drawings of it in various Egyptian temples and, above all, because of its unusual circumstances. The forward line of the Egyptian army was divided in two. The Hittites surrounded the vanguard, which was

Painted limestone statue of a priest of Amon dating from the twentieth dynasty

led by the pharaoh himself. The Egyptians managed to survive but it appears obvious that the battle was inconclusive.

The wars that followed produced no real change in their relative positions of power. In 1269 BC, Ramses II and the Hittite king Hattusili III made peace. The official text, called Eternal Treaty, is written on silver plaques in both Egyptian and Hittite. The two kings agreed not to attack or plunder each other's countries, to surrender political

refugees, and to act as military allies in case of invasion. This stipulation suggests the most urgent reason for concluding this alliance: the threat from other powers in the Near East. The Eternal Treaty was announced in Egypt with great pride, as if it were a victory. Its tone indicates that the habit of viewing foreign peoples as inferior, common in Egypt since the Old Kingdom, had become somewhat obsolete. Ramses II began to incorporate large numbers of Hittite divisions in his army, as he had done previously with the Libyans and Nubians. The treaty was ratified by an international marriage. Ramses took a daughter of the Hittite king as his wife.

There was also regular correspondence, excavated from the Hittite capital. It indicates that the kings and queens exchanged gifts. In one letter, King Hattusili III asked for Egyptian physicians and medicines to cure his eye ailment and his sister's infertility.

Over his long reign, Ramses took the opportunity to have significant work done on the country's temples. He had the temple of Luxor expanded and finished the great hypostyle hall begun by his father in the Temple of Amon at Karnak. He also finished Seti's temple at Abydos and made extensive donations to its domain. He built his own "million-year" (a common Egyptian description) temple in Abydos in addition to the Ramesseum, an enormous mortuary temple in Thebes.

He had new sanctuaries constructed in Nubia with colossal statues of himself. The rock-hewn temple of Abu Simbel is the best known. He was worshiped there, together with Amon, Re, and Ptah. He had a rock-cut temple dedicated to the goddess Hathor and his most important wife, Queen Nefertari. He enlarged his residence, *Pi-Ramesse* (House of Ramses), in the eastern Nile Delta. (This may be the place referred to as Ramesis in Exodus 1:11.)

The End of the Nineteenth Dynasty
Reports from the reign of Pharaoh Merneptah (1224–1214 BC), son and successor of Ramses II, show that Egypt's problems had not ended with the wars of his predecessor. Although peace had been made with the Hittites, other tribes still threatened the country's borders. The Libyans had become increasingly dangerous.

There was a new threat from the north, called the Sea Peoples. The Egyptians used this name for a number of groups that menaced the eastern Mediterranean coast from the Aegean. Among them were the Philistines, who settled in the area around Gaza in the thirteenth century BC. Merneptah seems to have been able to ward off the

Painted
wooden statue
of the god
Osiris

Relief on a limestone
pyramideon dating from
around 1250 BC,
showing the scribe Ramose
worshiping the sun god
Ra-Horakhte

attacks of all of these various groups. On a stele currently in the Egyptian Museum in Cairo, he recounts his victories.

These hieroglyphs also mention the people of Israel. The pharaoh claims that he has destroyed these people and that "their seed no longer exists." Because a number of major elements known from this period in Egypt are also described in the Old Testament, including the city of Ramesis, the Philistines, and the name Israel, it is possible that Merneptah was the pharaoh who, in the biblical account, after ten plagues, finally allowed the Jewish people to leave Egypt, pursuing them until his army was drowned in the Red Sea.

It was not developments abroad, but unrest within Egyptian borders that brought about the downfall of the nineteenth dynasty. Among a series of kings with brief reigns

187

On the side of the red granite sarcophagus of Ramses II, the goddess Isis spreads her wings to protect the mummy of the deceased pharaoh.

was Amenmesse, assumed to have ascended the throne unlawfully because later generations either omit him from history or simply refer to him as "the Enemy." A queen named Twosic ruled for two years, from 1198–1196 BC. An important behind-the-scenes role was played by the treasurer Bai, who, though not of royal blood, had a tomb carved for himself in the Valley of the Kings. He may be the foreigner referred to in the Harris Papyrus from the time of Ramses III, a Syrian called Irsu, which literally means "he who created himself." According to the same document, King Sethnakht finally brought this chaotic era to an end.

"Servants in the Place of Truth"

The workers of the royal tombs in the Valley of the Kings belonged to a work organization called "Servants in the Place of Truth." They were housed in an adjacent valley near the work site. Although their village was probably founded at the beginning of the New Kingdom, its houses are recognizable in the modern village on the same site, Deir el-Medina. Little is known of its inhabitants during the eighteenth dynasty, but an enormous number of texts from the time of the Ramesside kings has been preserved here,

Wooden writing board
with Egyptian characters dating
from the nineteenth dynasty
(ca. 1250 BC).
It clearly shows that
the Egyptians wrote from
right to left.

giving a lively account of the daily life of the workers. The *papyri* and *ostraca* (pieces of limestone with writing on them) from Deir el-Medina contain reports, lists of absentees, letters, contracts, invoices, wills, and other administrative records, as well as educational, literary, and magical texts. They describe a privileged group of artisans, building and decorating royal tombs on a full-time basis, who received their wages from the government in the form of rations. Their bosses were directly accountable to the vizier, who came to inspect their progress at regular intervals.

In addition to the work and its organization, the texts tell us much about the local economy and the trading, borrowing, and lending that took place among the villagers. All goods had fixed prices, expressed in quantities of grain or silver but paid in kind. Any dispute about the transactions could be submitted to the local council, where judgment was pronounced by a group of important villagers. The legal texts also provide an important insight into the position of women. More independent than women in other ancient societies, they were able to conclude agreements or institute legal proceedings without a male representative.

The Deir el-Medina texts also provide information about religion. People devoted much attention to the worship of their own ancestors and to small-scale local ceremonies.

Finally, the texts offer the earliest examples of a strike. When there were delays in the distribution of rations during and after the reign of Ramses III, the workers stopped working and marched in protest, sometimes with their entire families, to show their displeasure—and their hunger.

The Twentieth Dynasty

Sethnakht, the founder of the twentieth dynasty, was succeeded by Ramses III (1194–1163 BC). Since he tried to emulate his namesake Ramses II in everything, there is doubt as to the validity of his military victories depicted on the walls of his mortuary complex at Medinet Habu, near Thebes. There is no doubt, however, that he had to wage frequent wars, occasionally with success. Both the Libyans and the Sea Peoples were defeated during the eighth and eleventh years, respectively, of his reign.

We are well informed with regard to his domestic policies, particularly about his measures to expand and protect the temple domains. The Harris Papyrus lists the enormous gifts the king made to the temples of Thebes, Heliopolis, Memphis, and smaller cities. The document shows that the temples

Relief found during
excavations of the Temple of
Bubastis in the Nile Delta,
portraying Pharaoh Osorkon II
and his wife about
910 BC

189

The temple
of Ramses II in
Abu Simbel

Osiris on his throne,
from the relief on a priest's
sarcophagus of the
Saitic period,
around 600 BC

190

collectively were sent a large share of the country's agricultural and handcrafted products, but this was probably true of other periods as well. After the death of Ramses III, the kingdom began to decline.

Another papyrus, from the reign of Ramses V, shows that the temples were major owners and users of land. The priests and officials, who ultimately profited from the temple proceeds, achieved a rather independent position. The accumulation of wealth in the temples helped to weaken royal power. It seems likely that the kingdom's decline was accelerated by the priests. The Deir el-Medina texts show the high priest of Amon becoming ever more powerful in Thebes at the expense of the king.

Another important factor was the army. Expanded with troops that included foreign mercenaries, the army warded off attacks from abroad. The maintenance of this large military was only partially successful. Reports of Libyan troops preventing the members of "Servants in the Place of Truth" from performing their work implies a mutiny by some of the foreign soldiers.

The increasing power of both the priests of Amon and the army put an end to the New Kingdom around 1070 BC. A crisis arose in Thebes. The king sent his "Prince of Kush," Panehsi, to Thebes to dispose of the high priest of Amon. Panehsi appears to have regarded this as an opportunity to seize power in the area. General Piankh ordered in the royal troops to restore order. The chaos was well illustrated in a remark by General Piankh in a letter: "As for Pharaoh: how can he reach this land? And over whom does Pharaoh rule?"

Another general, Herihor, eventually became not only the commanding general himself, but also the high priest of Amon. These combined functions now made him the counterpart in Thebes of Pharaoh Ramses XI, last of the dynasty, who looked on helplessly from his distant residence in the Nile Delta.

Third Intermediate Period (Twenty-First through Twenty-Fourth Dynasties)

The twenty-first dynasty began the Third Intermediate period (1070–712 BC), characterized by opposing spheres of influence, pharaohs from Tanis in the north and high priests from Thebes in the south.

The relations between these regions were not purely hostile. The pharaoh was represented in Thebes by his daughter, the divine wife of Amon. The women assuming these positions were not the wives of successors to the throne. These women remained celibate, considering themselves married to the god Amon. Thebes became a separate state, the

"Divine State of Amon," guided by the high priests and the wives of the gods. As such, it continued to exist, even when the rest of Egypt was defeated by other nations.

Small Libyan principalities had arisen in the Nile Delta, some of which formed royal dynasties. The first king of Libyan descent was Shoshenk I (945–924 BC) (the biblical Sisak), founder of the twenty-first dynasty,

The god Osiris, as he appears in a mural in the tomb of Prince Amenherkhepeshef (ca. 1250 BC) in the Valley of the Queens near Thebes, where the pharaoh's relatives were buried

191

who had come to power as general of the Egyptian army. Libyans also began the twenty-second dynasty challenged by contemporary rivals of the twenty-third and twenty-fourth dynasties.

The Late Period (Twenty-Fifth through Thirtieth Dynasties)

The Libyan domination was ended by the Kushites, founders of the twenty-fifth dynasty who had built a powerful kingdom south of Egypt (in what is called Sudan today). They ruled from 712 BC until they were expelled by the Assyrians in 664.

The Syrians brought an Egyptian puppet king to the throne in 672 BC. This king, Nekho, managed to secede from the Syrian Empire. Under his successor, Psamtik I of the twenty-sixth dynasty, Egypt experienced its last era of independence and even a cultural resurgence under native kings.

Part of this renewed interest in cultural matters was literary. About 700 BC, demotic Egyptian replaced the Late Egyptian language introduced in the eighteenth dynasty. This new demotic (or "popular") Egyptian was now accepted as the standard for literature. Written in its own unique demotic script, the literary language seems to have been patterned after the spoken forms prevalent at the same time. It was the Egyptian standard as the country fell under first Persian, then Greek, and finally Roman domination. Coptic, considered the last of five versions of the Egyptian language, would begin to replace it about AD 300. The written form of Coptic, based on an adaptation of Greek letters, would replace demotic script. Although still used in religious texts and the Coptic church, spoken Coptic yielded to Arabic about AD 700 and virtually disappeared by the fourteenth century.

Egypt was unable to stand up against the steadily expanding power of the immense Persian Empire. Cambyses II defeated the Egyptian pharaoh in 525 BC, placing the country under the Persian domination of the twenty-seventh dynasty. Native Egyptian rulers reasserted their independence in the next three dynasties, but the thirtieth was the last. Manetho does not list the thirty-first dynasty, the return to Persian domination. This time it would hold until the conquest of Egypt by Alexander the Great in 332 made the country part of the Greek world.

It would be a mistake to consider this long period of foreign domination as a time of social or cultural decline. Although it lost its political independence for centuries, Egypt continued to exert profound influence on other societies.

Long before Alexander's conquest of Egypt in 332 BC, the Greeks had been looking to Egypt for inspiration. Many experts believe that two of the hallmarks of Greek art and architecture—the creation of life-sized and even larger sculptures and the use of high, stone columns with decorated capitals—were begun in imitation of the construction and decoration of ancient Egyptian temples.

Papyrus with proverbs and emblems from the Book of the Dead, dating from the late New Kingdom

Bronze statue inlaid with electrum and silver, representing Queen Karomama, wife to Pharaoh Takalot II of the twenty-second dynasty (ca. 850 BC)

192

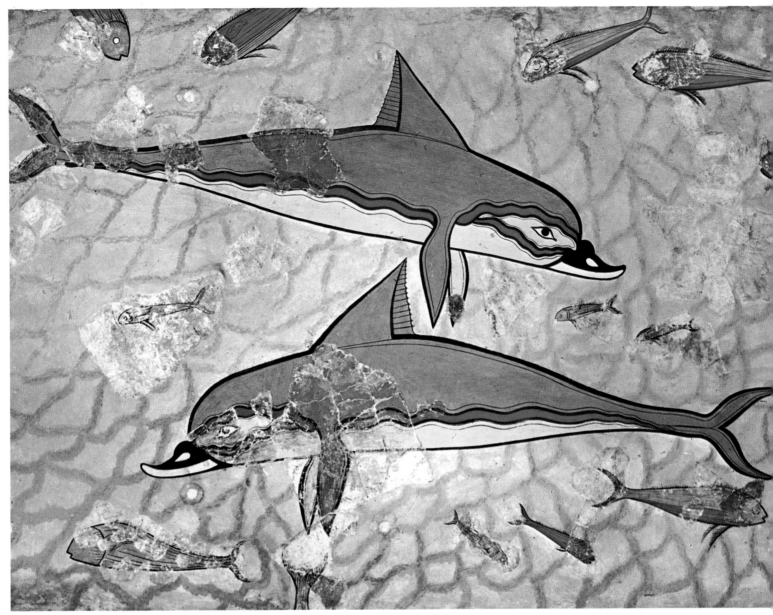

Restored fresco, the so-called Dolphin Fresco, from a floor in the palace at Knossos (1500-1450 BC)

The Minoan Civilization

The Rise and Flowering of a Bronze Age Civilization on Crete

Crete is the fifth largest island in the Mediterranean Sea, constituting both a region of present-day Greece and the largest island of its archipelago. One hundred and fifty miles (241.3 kilometers) long and thirty-five miles (56.3 kilometers) across at its widest, it is largely mountainous. Its highest mountains are in the west, where peaks in the Lévka Óri range reach 7,500 feet (2,290 meters). Those in the eastern region are generally under 5,000 feet (1,524 meters). Most of the coastline is steep and inaccessible except on the island's northern coast, where there are several harbors. The population has always concentrated there and in the few arable valleys and plains. The Mesara plain in southern central Crete is extremely large by Greek standards, with a length of twenty-four miles (38.6 kilometers). Yet because of its favorable climate and many springs and rivers,

193

An example of a Cycladic marble idol, found on the isle of Paros. This particular type of idol is known as a "folded-arms figure" and dates from the early third millennium BC.

Crete was a rich agricultural area as early as the Bronze Age. Of particular relevance to its culture is the large number of caves.

In antiquity, the island looked different than it does today. The mountains were covered with trees, especially oak, cypress, olive, and fir, and palms grew on the plains. Even before the deforestation of the nineteenth and twentieth centuries, erosion produced bare hills and reshaped the valleys where the eroded soil was deposited. During the Bronze Age, erosion was not a major problem, but then, as now, there was the permanent threat of earthquakes. It may have been an earthquake that damaged the palace of Knossos in 1700 BC, punctuating an epoch in the island's history.

Earliest History

Although nothing has been found on Crete that indisputably dates from the Paleolithic Age, the region was undoubtedly inhabited in the Neolithic Age. The oldest-known settlements of Neolithic farmers, found in Thessaly and Macedonia in northern Greece and in Knossos on Crete, date from around

An example of a specific type of pottery from the Cyclades known as the "Cycladic frying pan," dating from the third millennium BC

6500 to 5500 BC. The first people who colonized the area may have come from Asia Minor. We can be sure that Crete was part of a network of contacts spanning the entire Aegean area. During the Late Neolithic period, the southern portion of the Aegean territory became more important: The Cyclades and the more remote parts of Crete were now being settled. During the Bronze Age, which began in approximately 3000 BC, the cultural center moved to the south. Three separate cultures of Aegean civilization came into being, each with their own specific character. The Minoan culture developed on Crete while the Cycladic originated in the northern archipelago called the Cyclades. On the Greek mainland, Helladic culture arose. Its final stages are known as the Mycenaean civilization.

A Mythical Past

The discovery of these old civilizations is fairly recent. Not until the beginning of this century did the soil of Crete release its secrets. The Greeks of the Classic era recorded vague memories of a culture that had once flourished on Crete, albeit in a mythical form. According to Greek mythology, the god Poseidon sent a snow-white bull to the mighty King Minos for sacrifice to him. When the king refused, the god made Pasiphaë, the wife of Minos and the queen of Crete, fall in love with the bull. The offspring she bore as a result, a monster with a human body and a bull's head, is called the Minotaur. King Minos had the architect Daedalus build a labyrinth so complex that nobody could find his way through it. Minos had the Minotaur locked inside and fed it the humans he required Athens to provide him as tribute. The hero Theseus decided to put an end to this and offered himself as a victim. Ariadne, the daughter of Minos, fell in love with Theseus and found him a way to escape. She gave him a ball of thread, which he tied at the entrance to the maze and unwound as he went. He beat the sleeping Minotaur to death and followed the thread back with victims he had rescued.

This myth apparently recalls a bull cult on Crete and its large complicated buildings, the "palaces" dating from the Bronze Age. The word *labyrinth* literally means "the house with the double ax." Several examples of double axes, apparently cult objects, have been found on Crete.

Arthur Evans's Excavations

The discovery of Cretan civilization must largely be credited to Arthur John Evans (AD 1851-1941), who became Sir Arthur Evans in 1911. In 1900, Evans started to excavate Knossos at his own expense. His curiosity had been first aroused by samples of an unknown script, which originated from the Greek mainland and Crete. Gradually, he became convinced that this script was part of a major Cretan civilization, which he called Minoan after Minos.

Based on his findings, Evans drew up a chronology distinguishing three main

Rhyton (drinking cup) shaped like a bull and dating from the Bronze Age

periods: Early Minoan (3000-2000 BC), Middle Minoan (2000-1600 BC), and Late Minoan (1600-1050 BC). He divided each of these three main periods into three stages. This division is still employed by archaeologists, but historically the following division is more useful: the period prior to the palaces (3000-1900 BC), the First Palace period (1900-1700 BC), the Second Palace period (1650-1450 BC), the Third Palace period (1450 to 1200 BC) and the Post-Palace period (1200-1000 BC). These time spans, not defined by Evans, but based on recent findings, provide only a rough outline. Absolute dates are based on Egyptian objects found on Crete or on Cretan objects found in Egypt, since we know a lot more about Egyptian history. Scientific methods like carbon-14 dating have also been used. There is considerable deviation in the results of the two methods of dating. Sufficient uncertainty exists to allow ample room for debate.

Crete as a Center of Trade

Crete had commercial relations with the Aegean and Cycladic islands, the Greek mainland, Asia Minor (Turkey), Cyprus, Egypt, and the Canaanite Syrian coast. Through intermediaries, its contacts reached even further: Documents in cuneiform script from the eighteenth century BC originating in Mari, a city along the Euphrates River in Syria, mention various products from Kaptara (probably Crete) which were transported via Ugarit on the Syrian coast.

These contacts started early, but increased during the First and Second Palace periods. Especially during the second, there was intensive exchange between the Minoan culture and the rest of the world. Starting in the fifteenth century BC, Egyptian sources regularly depict people called the *Keftiu*, undoubtedly the Minoan Cretans. The archaeological finds from Crete include many objects from the Near East. Conversely,

The throne room in the palace of Knossos, where the original Minoan throne is still located along the wall

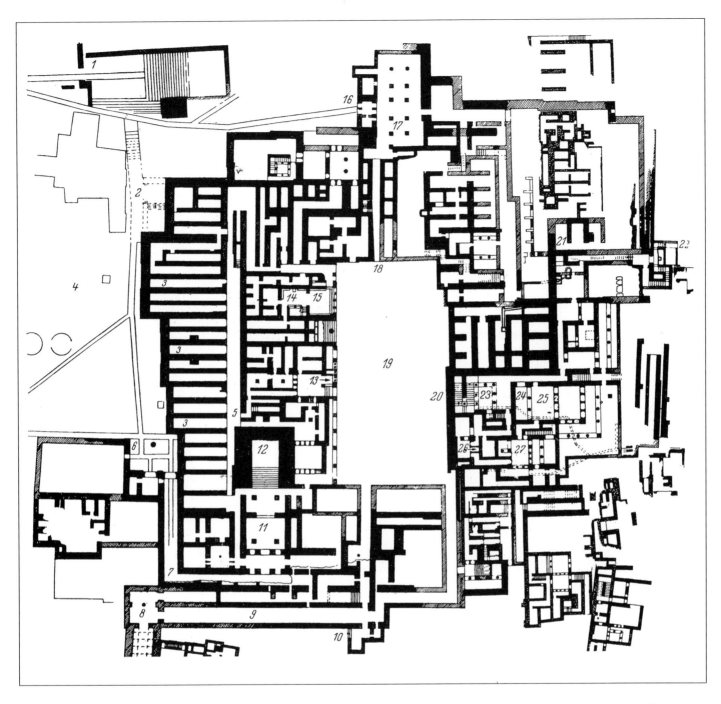

Minoan objects have been found in many other places.

During the Third Palace period, trade became still more international. A shipwreck from this period, the *Ulu Burun*, was found to contain Egyptian, Mesopotamian, Syro-Palestinian, Cypriot, Mycenaean, and Minoan products. There were objects from other parts of Europe as well. During this period, Mycenae played the main role, although a considerable part of the Mycenaean trade passed through Crete. Even after 1200 BC, when international trade began to decline, Cretan ties with the Near East never completely disappeared. Crete's central place in Mediterranean trade is undeniable. This is an extensive Minoan sphere of influence, although not necessarily one accompanied by political or military power. It is unlikely that a large Minoan maritime empire ever existed.

Plan of the palace in Knossos 1. Broad staircase for official entry 2. Northwestern stairs 3. Rooms for storage 4. Western inner court 5. Corridor alongside the storage rooms 6. Entrance hall 7. Corridor decorated with frescoes of a procession 8. Southwestern entrance 9. Southern corridor 10. Southern entrance 11. Vestibule of the main stairwell 12. Main staircase 13. Sanctuary 14. Throne hall 15. Front room to the throne hall 16. Northern entrance 17. Large hall with columns 18. Passageway to the main inner court 19. Inner court 20. Stairwells leading to the living quarters 21. Storeroom with large *pithoi* (storage jars) 22. Eastern bastion 23. Collonade 24. Hall without a roof 25. Hall of the Double Axes 26. Toilet 27. The queen's boudoir

The First Palace Period

The first palaces were completed after 2000 BC, often from earlier starts. They include Knossos, Phaestos in the Mesara plain,

197

Olive oil, olives, wine, and grain were kept in large jars and amphoras and stored in special storage rooms. These are some of the storage jars in the palace at Knossos.

Mallia twenty-five miles (40 kilometers) east of Knossos on the northern coast –and Zakro (on the east coast). The term *palace* is used to include the complex of settlements that surrounded the great edifices. The palaces served as storage places for agricultural products, as workshops for artisans and artists, and as the island's administrative centers. It is not clear whether the palace settlements were independent principalities or parts of a federation led by the largest of them, the centrally located Knossos.

The first palaces have disappeared almost completely. There are, however, numerous finds from the first period. One of the most striking of these is a type of refined pottery, sometimes extremely thin-walled, known as Kamares ware pottery. Most of it is ceramic turned on a pottery wheel. It is decorated with spirals and plant motifs in red, orange, yellow, and white on a blue-black background. This high-quality Kamares pottery

was undoubtedly crafted by specialized potters for both the domestic market and export.

We can form a fairly good idea of the architecture of this period from a collection of small plaques found in the palace of Knossos. Made of *faience*, a fine grade of pottery with a glaze, these depict city houses made of masonry bound with large wooden beams. All have at least two floors. Several window openings are painted bright red on the faience images. This might indicate the use of oiled parchment or some other precursor of windowpanes. All the houses have flat roofs, and many display a type of central tower, possibly serving as an air and light shaft or as a summer bedroom.

A few terra-cotta figurines from the period 2000 to 1700 BC give us an idea of the way these Cretans looked. One of these is the statue of a man found in a mountain sanctuary on the east coast of Crete. His skin is the same color as that of Egyptian statues, red or dark brown. He wears only a loincloth and a sash, tied tightly around his waistline, perhaps to accentuate it. An accompanying statue of a woman has skin of pale white, again the same color as in Egyptian specimens. The woman's statue is remarkable for its clothing. A long skirt falls to her feet; a narrow bodice leaves her breasts bare. Her hair is piled high on her head. With minor changes, these fashions were maintained for centuries.

Seals are an important source of information on Minoan culture. An entire archive of them has been found at Phaistos since AD 1900. Seals were in common use for placing a personal or official stamp as a signature on certain objects. They were also used as ornaments and amulets. Their designs consist not only of geometric patterns, but also of representations of human beings and animals, including such legendary beasts as the griffin and the sphinx. After 1900 BC, the seals bear a type of writing that Sir Arthur Evans termed *hieroglyphic*. Two and a half centuries later, this was replaced by a simplified syllabic script called Linear A, not yet deciphered. It has been found inked on stone and pottery vessels. Seals were used to stamp a series of symbols on both sides of a unique clay disk, also found at Phaistos, that may constitute the earliest printed text.

The Second Palace Period

Around 1700 BC, the first flowering of the Minoan civilization came to a gradual end. An earthquake has often been posited as the reason, but despite the many signs of earthquake damage on Crete, a catastrophe occurring simultaneously throughout the island is unlikely. Internal war is another possible cause. In any case, the decline was temporary, immediately followed by a revival, the period of the new palaces beginning around 1650 BC. During it, the large complexes at Knossos, Phaistos, Zakro, and Mallia were rebuilt. The palace at Knossos was made far more elaborate, at least three stories high with many rooms, most notably, the magnificent throne room. The kings of Knossos attained the peak of their power about 1550 to 1500 BC, dominating the Aegean region and trading extensively with Egypt.

The ruins of the palaces remain an impressive testimony to the Minoan civilization. The palace at Knossos was the first to be excavated. Perhaps, unfortunately, it was somewhat rigorously restored—not to say reconstructed —by Arthur Evans. Later on, the palace at Phaistos was brought to light by Italian excavations, the Mallia palace was unearthed by a French expedition, and Zakro was discovered by the Greeks themselves.

Detail of a fresco in the Corridor of the Procession and the south Propylaeum of the palace at Knossos, depicting a procession of people bearing offerings (1500-1450 BC)

Rhyton (drinking cup) made of steatite, inlaid with limestone and rock crystal. The horns are covered with gold leaf. These horns were found in the so-called Little Palace at Knossos, and measure 18 inches (45 centimeters) (1600-1300 BC).

199

Restored fresco
from the palace of Knossos,
portraying a number of
ladies-in-waiting

Gold signet ring, found
in a grave near Knossos and
made around 1500 BC.
Four women are performing a
religious dance, while a
god appears in the
background.

200

The palaces are built according to a single basic pattern with minor adaptations. Rectangular inner courtyards are located in the center. Although the palaces were built outward from these courtyards, they were not closed off from the outside. The western facades opened on wide *agoras* (public courtyards for ceremonies and gatherings) and often had a number of windows next to the entrance gate.

The other rooms of the palace, clustered around the inner courtyards, included storerooms, reception halls, living quarters, and artisans' workshops. These four types of rooms are found in each palace, separated by long corridors, usually perpendicular or parallel to the inner courtyard. The enormous storerooms are striking. They contain rows of man-sized ceramic vats called *pithoi* for storing grain, oil, and wine. There is evidence of a system of weights and measures. Below the floor are stone cellars that can be closed with large hatches. The use of many other rooms, especially the living quarters and the reception halls, is disputed, because we know so little about the inhabitants. Many questions remain unanswered about

the structure and function of the Minoan palaces.

We should imagine these palaces as being encircled by large cities. In Zakro, a luxurious town with paved streets and large houses was excavated before the palace was discovered. Other urban settlements have been excavated that were not located near any of the major palaces; Gournia in eastern Crete is a famous example. Here a settlement was found complete with dwellings and workshops. This means that the oldest cities on European soil were in ancient Crete.

Crete is also strewn with excavated villas built on the same plan as the palaces. A large villa is hard to distinguish from a small palace. In fact, the palace of Hagia Triada is sometimes referred to as a villa. Archanes, seven miles (11.3 kilometers) from Knossos, is also a villa of this type. It is assumed to have served as an adjunct to the large palace in Phaistos, only a few miles (5 kilometers) away. In the middle of Gournia, there is a villa facing an area that probably served as a market square for the entire town. Possibly the villas were the regional official seats of a central power. This hypothesis is

supported by the nature of the finds, including examples of the Linear A script and by the distance between the villas, about seven to ten miles (11.3 to 16.1 kilometers).

Murals and Other Art Forms

The interiors of the new palaces, especially Knossos, were brightened with colorful murals elegantly depicting abstract patterns such as spirals, plants, animals, and people. These paintings are often called frescoes, but they were painted on dry plaster walls, unlike true frescoes, which are painted on wet plaster. The paintings of plants are probably the oldest. Later artists began to paint landscapes with animals. The House of the Frescoes at Knossos is famous; its murals show a park where various flowering plants are complemented by high-spouting fountains and a blue bird. Frescoes with dolphins and flying fish have been found in several places.

There is a clear evolution from miniature

A view of the palace at Phaistos, looking north. In the foreground are the domestic quarters immediately east of the central court.

The so-called horns of consecration on the south front of the palace of Knossos. These are stylized bull's horns with a ritual significance.

frescoes to life-sized or more than life-sized images of men and women. The spontaneity and emotion with which the artists rendered these figures gives them great charm even today. These paintings are where we get to know the Cretans—perhaps not the way they actually were, but certainly how they wanted to be. We see slim, tan men with narrow hips and broad shoulders wearing loincloths, and elegant, white-skinned women with their wide skirts, curly hair, carefully applied makeup, and bare breasts. Often the women occupy a prominent position in the frescoes. Painted with great detail, they are shown dominating ceremonies from a place of honor, for example, or they are performing dances in beautiful costumes.

Large statuary from the Minoan civilization is virtually unknown, but the pedestals of presumably wooden statues have been preserved. A number of small statues have been found, made of ivory (sometimes inlaid with gold), bronze, and faience. They depict goddesses or priestesses, praying figures, acrobats, animals, and a few tableaus, such as a stable with cattle or a group of dancers. Sometimes children are portrayed.

The ceramics from this period bear witness to great technical and artistic traditions. An enormous variety of motifs from the plant kingdom evolves out of the Kamares style. Octopuses and other marine animals are used to decorate pottery. These decorations are painted in dark colors against a light back-

ground; the technique of the Kamares style was the exact opposite. We find here the same lively motion that characterized the art of the frescoes. During the final period, a certain rigidity arises as the same motifs are put in stricter order. Stone, ceramic, and gold objects also show a great refinement. In this luxurious world, the tradition of costly, elegant golden jewelry naturally continued. Numerous seal stones with engraved images are of particular interest as one of our best sources of knowledge of religious life.

Religion

We do not know much about Cretan religion. The ceremonies took place in the open air, sometimes on mountain peaks or in caves. Few buildings have been found that can be identified as temples, but the palaces contain many rooms which might have served that purpose. Traces have been found of sacrifices and votive offerings, often the small statues mentioned above, sometimes representing people in an attitude of prayer. From the images, we can conclude that there were processions and dances, priests and priestesses. The purpose of the rituals was probably to ensure fertility and ward off disaster.

Birds on a restored fresco from the visitor's room in the palace of Knossos (1700-1500 BC)

Restored fresco from the Knossos palace, known as the "Prince of Lilies" (1500-1450 BC)

203

ble axes, and bulls obviously occupied an important place. Trees occur in scenes portraying an epiphany, the visible manifestation of a deity on Earth. Snakes writhe in the hands of priestesses or goddesses. There are also remarkable depictions of an acrobatic game in which male and female adolescents perform cartwheels on the back of a bull.

It is certain that the sacrifices practiced on Crete included the slaughter of animals, but the Minoan religion may have had an even more dramatic side. In the mountains some four and a half miles (7.2 kilometers) south of Knossos, a major sanctuary was excavated in Anemospilia in 1979. Extremely interesting items were found, including what is probably a cult statue and a number of votive offerings. A further discovery was made which caused great excitement. When an earthquake destroyed the sanctuary some time during the first half of the seventeenth century BC, a human sacrifice had apparently been in progress. Experts in forensic medicine have convincingly proved that the body of a young man found tied to a low altar did not perish as a result of the earthquake. He had died slightly before it by bleeding to death after his carotid arteries (on each side of the neck) had been cut. In Knossos, the bones of children have been found that show knife marks suggesting child sacrifice or even ritual cannibalism. Several archaeological and textual indications support the idea that these were not isolated instances.

The Mycenaeans

Around 1450 BC, the palaces of the second period came to an abrupt end. The cause has often been sought in a large volcanic eruption that destroyed the island of Thera, but there is evidence that this eruption took place much earlier and caused only limited damage on Crete. Other possible causes include earthquakes, civil disturbance, and invasion by people from the Greek mainland. Damage from earthquakes can indeed be demonstrated in a number of cases, but elsewhere the destruction seems to be caused by man. It is not certain that this was the work of invaders. The arrival of Greek-speaking Mycenaeans from the mainland may have been a result rather than a cause.

The palace at Knossos, which had suffered relatively little damage, again became an administrative center for a major part of the island, this time under foreign domination. But by 1300 BC, it appears to have been destroyed by unknown attackers. Minoan culture began its long decline as Mycenaean civilization began to flourish. The coincidence suggests the purposeful destruction of Minoan civilization by the Mycenaeans.

Gold cup, made on Crete between 1500 and 1450 BC and found in a grave near Vaphio. The decoration on this so-called second Vaphio Cup is a picture of a bull that is caught and tethered by its hind leg.

Many sanctuaries in the open were later associated with Zeus, so it is possible that the god to whom they were originally dedicated bore certain similarities to Zeus. Other sanctuaries within the palaces were used to worship a mother goddess, probably the Greek Rhea. Associated with her worship was the double ax, executed in all shapes and materials and clearly related to religion, possibly also as the horns of bulls. Trees, snakes, dou-

Detail of the access gate to the fortress of Mycenae, the so-called Lion Gate (fourteenth century BC)

Mycenae

The First Flowering of Civilization on the Greek Mainland

About 1600 BC, a culture began to develop on the Greek mainland similar in many respects to the Minoan culture on Crete, yet with enough difference to deserve its own separate place in history. Part of the Late Helladic civilization of the Bronze Age, it is called the Mycenaean culture, after the ancient city which was one of its centers.

Mycenae lies on the plain of Argolis, in the northeast region of the Greek Peninsula called the Peloponnisos. Mycenae reached its peak as the center of Aegean civilization about 1400. It continued to expand between 1400 and 1200, undermining Minoan dominance of the region and coinciding with the Third Palace period of Minoan culture.

205

The language of the Mycenaean culture was identified as an early Greek dialect only in AD 1952. Thousands of clay tablets inscribed with its script, called Linear B, had been found at Pylos and Mycenae on the Greek mainland and on Crete. Dating from about 1400 to 1150 BC, they had been excavated over a period of years after AD 1900, but were not deciphered until half a century later by Michael Ventris and John Chadwick. Other tablets found with them are inscribed with another script called Linear A, still not deciphered. These date from as early as 1750 BC and are known to be from the earlier Minoan culture.

The discovery that Linear B was a form of Greek rather than a separate language of the Minoans was a great surprise to many scholars. It initiated a search for the "first Greeks," discrediting the once-popular migration theory that Greek-speaking people had entered the region and established the Greek language and culture in approximately 2000 BC. It is generally accepted that such people did migrate to the Peloponnisos about that time, if not sooner. They probably arrived in small groups and lived in close proximity with indigenous tribes speaking other languages. They are considered unlikely to have produced a sudden change in population and culture. Greek may have been the language of only a small elite. The fact now established that it was used in the palaces during the Mycenaean era does not mean that everyone spoke it. Greek culture was already in full swing elsewhere during this era and would be long after the Mycenaeans declined.

The Excavations of Heinrich Schliemann

The *Iliad,* the heroic epic dating from the eighth century BC and ascribed to a poet named Homer, describes Mycenae as the paramount city in the Greek world. He tells of its king Agamemnon; his brother Menelaus, king of Sparta; and the rulers Nestor of

Mycenaean
terra-cotta figurine
depicting a
goddess

Bronze dagger with a gold hilt. The blade is inlaid with a silver decoration of leopards hunting. It was probably made on Crete and found in the palace of Pylos.

Pylos and Odysseus of Ithaca. All of them took part in the Trojan War, the ten-year siege of the city of Troy in westernmost Turkey. Another epic, the *Odyssey*, tells of Odysseus's wanderings on his return to Ithaca after the war.

Both of these epics were once regarded as primarily fictional, at best reflecting the later Greek culture of their origin. Our ability to interpret them as history is a relatively recent development. The opinion generally accepted today is that the *Iliad* and *Odyssey* describe the Mycenaean world of the period following the Bronze Age, known as the Dark Age, from the tenth to the ninth centuries BC.

One hundred and twenty-five years ago, nothing was known about Greek history prior to 800 BC. The change is due to the work of the German Heinrich Schliemann (AD 1822-1890). In much the manner that Arthur Evans uncovered the early history of Crete, Schliemann unearthed the Mycenaean culture, driven by the idea that Homer had described an historic reality in Asia Minor. Although we now view the historic reality of the Homeric epic very differently from Schliemann, his work triggered a series of discoveries that dramatically changed our image of history. A few weeks after - Schliemann began the excavations of Mycenae, he uncovered a grave that contained exquisite golden objects. A death mask, a golden replica of the features of the deceased, made a deep impression on him. "Today, I stood face to face with Agamemnon," he wired to King George of Greece.

The fortress of Mycenae dominated the city and the surrounding area. In contrast to the palaces on Crete, the Mycenaean fortresses were fortified with thick walls against possible attacks.

The conclusion was premature. The death mask is anonymous, but the deep impression remained.

Schliemann was an amateur adventurer-archaeologist and a brilliant egocentric. His reports, especially where they concern himself, are often considered untrustworthy. Schliemann spent the fortune he earned in business on his dream of proving the truth of Homer's epics. For the most part, he proceeded relatively conscientiously and thoroughly by the standards of his time. Though not a professional archaeologist, he was far more than a simple treasure hunter. Starting in AD 1871, he excavated a city in the hill of Hissarlik in western Turkey, considered the site of Homer's Troy since ancient times. After 1876, he worked in Mycenae. Here, identification offered no problems. Mycenae's ruins were identified and described in the travel guide written by Pausanias in the second century AD. Schliemann used it to find the city's oldest layers of habitation.

The Early History of Mycenae

Mycenae was an important center during the sixteenth century BC, where rich graves were dug for its kings, but the town had been inhabited far earlier. Earthenware pieces have been preserved that date back to the Early Helladic period (2100 BC). Beautiful ceramics and paintings from the Middle Helladic period have been found. An extensive burial ground from the end of that period is located below the site where the Lion Gate and the southwest wall of the Mycenaean citadel were later built. These opulent royal tombs, discovered by Schliemann, were built in the early sixteenth century BC. This site is currently called Grave Circle A to distinguish it from a second grave circle, Grave Circle B, which was discovered in AD 1952 and excavated over the next two years. Grave Circle B lies outside the walls of the citadel and was not dug until

A portion of the walls of the fortress Mycenae. Impressed with the enormous stones from which the walls were built, Greeks from later times coined the expression "Cyclopean Walls." In Greek mythology, Cyclops were giants with one eye in the middle of their forehead. The Greeks called the stonework Cyclopean because only a giant could lift such large stones.

Hexagonal wooden box, covered with little plates of chased gold. It was made in the sixteenth century BC and found in one of the shaft graves in Mycenae.

208

Linear B

At Knossos, Arthur Evans found the first clay tablets inscribed with letters that resembled those on the seal stones that had inspired him to undertake his excavations. Over 3,000 such tablets have been found on Crete since AD 1900. There appeared to be three distinct types of script, which Evans called hieroglyphic (the oldest form), Linear A, and Linear B. He himself did not succeed in deciphering this material. In 1939, excavations at a Mycenaean palace in Pylos on the Peloponnisos turned up many more Linear B tablets. These were published in 1951. Since then, more have been found at Mycenae, Tiryns, and Thebes. With the materials from Pylos and Knossos, Michael Ventris, an amateur, was able to decipher the Linear B script. Everyone still believed that the script represented the unknown language of the Minoans because the letters of Linear B were clearly based on those of Linear A. Ventris did not assume that the tablets would contain Greek. He tried to establish a phonetic value for the syllabic letters based on assumptions about the place names on the tablets. Starting from such names as Konoso and Aminiso (later Knossos and Amnissos), he was able to uncover an archaic form of Greek. In 1953, together with John Chadwick, a specialist in Greek historical linguistics, Ventris published his first results in a controversial article. His decipherment has now been generally accepted.

Linear B tablet found in the palace of Knossos (fourteenth century BC). The first Linear B tablets were discovered at the end of the last century, but the writing was only deciphered in AD 1952.

the seventeenth century BC. It was used simultaneously with Grave Circle A.

The fabulous treasures that accompanied the deceased display the power and wealth of Mycenae in those days. The shaft burials of Grave Circles A and B yielded gold death masks and richly decorated weapons. The blades of a number of the daggers Schliemann discovered in Grave Circle A are inlaid with gold, silver, or alloys. Entire scenes are depicted in inlay work and often feature hunts and battles. The hilts of these daggers are often made of wood or bone to which reliefs of hammered gold were applied. The deceased were not only provided with weapons, however. Splendid utensils have been found in the burial shafts: vases, dishes, golden *rhytons* (drinking vessels), beautifully crafted diadems, earrings, hairpins, necklaces, and bracelets, as well as hundreds of tiny golden disks, which probably served to adorn clothes. The signet rings and cylinder seals from the graves are among the most beautiful this civilization has left.

The tomb findings bear testimony to Mycenae's extensive contact with the outside world, especially with Minoan Crete. The nature of this contact has not yet been explained, nor has the sudden wealth of the Mycenaean elite. It may have come from trade, from warfare, or from piracy. These were often not separate activities. At any rate, the end of the Middle Helladic era produced a general increase in prosperity among the elite on the Greek mainland, evident in its burial rituals.

Tombs and their findings play an important role in the picture of Mycenae. In the Mycenaean world, important tombs were usually richly supplied with grave offerings. The shape of the tombs varies. In addition to tombs, pits, shafts, and mounds, there are also burial chambers of various kinds. Their common feature is an underground room and an uncovered access path, the *dromos*. Many burial chambers were hewn from rock, but a special shape appears to have been reserved for the elite, the domed chamber, or *tholos*. Heinrich Schliemann excavated many of them between AD 1876 and 1878. He called them the beehive tombs. They are known locally as the Treasury of Atreus and the Tomb of Clytemnestra. The burial space consists of a round hole in the ground, covered by a dome of stone blocks. The blocks were laid in such a way that each layer protruded inward over the layer below, leaving only a small opening at the top. This was closed with an apex stone. The stone blocks were covered with soil and pebbles to increase pressure on them. The mound thus created was given an identifying mark or gravestone. Inside, the protruding portions of the stone blocks were removed, and the surface was smoothed, creating a conical dome. Smaller stone burial chambers also exist similar to the tholos. Most of the domed graves date from Crete's second palace period, but even after 1450 BC, they were still being built.

The Third Palace Period at Mycenae

The beginning of an entirely new period in the architectural history of Mycenae's palaces and fortresses is marked in 1450 BC. Architecture at Mycenae reaches great heights during the Late Helladic or Mycenaean period, to which the palace on

The entrance to the so-called Treasury of Atreus, a huge tomb, approximately 300 yards (274.3 meters) from the Mycenaean citadel (1300 BC)

Vessel made from rock crystal, shaped like a duck. It was found in the Grave Circle A in Mycenae and dates from the first half of the sixteenth century BC

210

the citadel, the enormous defensive walls, the underground vaults, the houses, and domed graves bear impressive testimony. Over a number of structural stages, an all but impregnable fortress would arise from a simple group of buildings. The fortress was seated on a plateau dominating the Argive plain and surrounded by a wall almost half a mile (80.5 meters) long and at least twenty feet (6.1 meters) thick. This wall, consisting of large limestone blocks, was made of a type of masonry called Cyclopean. The ancients believe that such heavy walls could only have been built by the Cyclops, enormous mythical giants. The wall carefully skirts Grave Circle A, perhaps considered a type of national sanctuary. This suggests an uninter-

rupted tradition at Mycenae since 1600 BC.

On the west side of the fortress is the Lion Gate, an impressive structure crowned by a relief depicting two lions standing on their hind legs on either side of a column. The gate was closed by a double door, indicated by the spindle holes above and below the threshold and lintel. From these holes protruded the spindle ends on which the doors were hung. They could also be shut from the inside by a cross beam, evident from the holes in the jambs. The threshold still shows traces of wear from chariots and carts.

The palace dominating the citadel lies at the center of the fortress, covering an area 200 by 180 feet (61 by 55 meters). It is built on uneven terrain, so that it probably gave

The so-called
Grave Circle A inside
the walls of the fortress at
Mycenae
(sixteenth century BC)

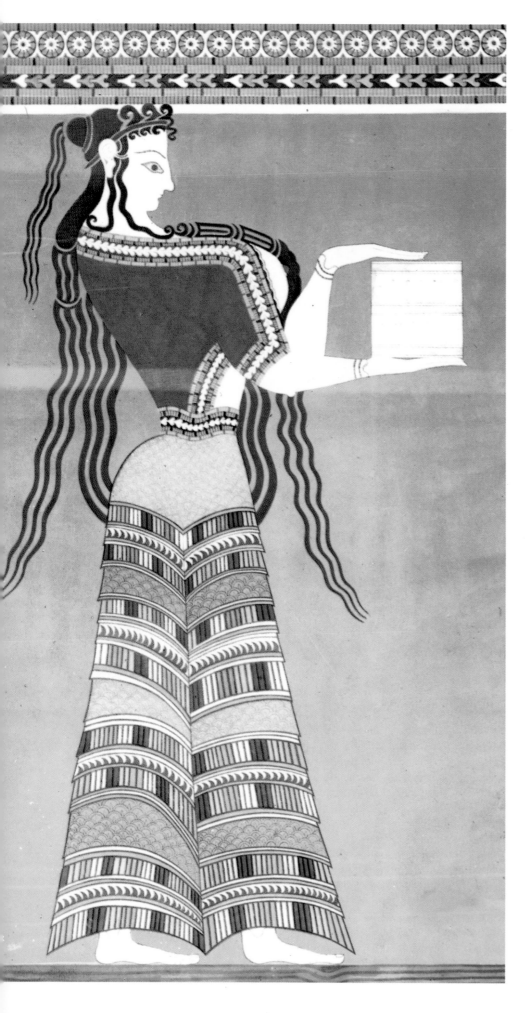

the impression of a stepped or terraced structure. The core of the complex is formed by the *megaron,* a rectangular room with a central hearth. The roof above the hearth had a round opening supported by four columns. The megaron had an entrance hall with columns in front, anticipating the shape of the later Greek temple. There are many differences between the Cretan and Mycenaean palaces, but certain aspects show a common influence. The wooden cross beam is also used in construction in Mycenae. Parts of the interior were painted or covered with stucco as they were at Knossos.

In addition to the king and his relatives, the citadel probably also housed a number of other noble families. Most of the houses were spacious and probably had two stories. Some of them may have served as annexes to the palace; some archaeologists assume that all the dwellings inside the walls were palace buildings. In the late 1960s, a sanctuary was found within the walls containing the remains of terra-cotta figures two feet (0.6 meters) high, possibly cult statues. Interesting murals display a Minoan influence. Recent excavations have brought to light a number of dwellings on the hillsides surrounding the citadel. A substantial town probably extended from the foot of the Cyclopean walls. A large portion of the surrounding population could have taken refuge within the citadel in times of war.

The citadel also contains the "Treasury of Atreus," which is actually an exceptionally handsome domed grave from the late fourteenth century BC. Its *dromos* is 120 feet (36.6 meters) long and twenty feet (6.1 meters) wide. The thirty-foot (9.1-meter) facade has been robbed of its decoration but is striking for its majestic size. A gigantic block weighing 120 tons (5,443 kilograms) closes off the top of the entrance, which is twenty feet (6.1 meters) deep. The dome has a diameter and height of approximately forty-five feet (13.7 meters). It consists of thirty-three layers of stone blocks fitted snugly together. Remnants of bronze nails suggest that the dome may well have been decorated, probably with bronze rosettes and friezes.

The World of the Mycenaeans
The Mycenaean culture was not confined to Mycenae. It extended throughout southern mainland Greece and to some of the islands.

Reconstruction of
a fresco from the fortress
of Tiryns (near Myceanae)
showing a woman
bearing offerings
(1300 BC)

A passageway
in the palace fortress
of Tiryns

A gold mask from a
shaft grave in Grave Circle A
at Mycenae, known
erroneously as "the Mask
of Agamemnon."
Its height is 12$\frac{1}{2}$ inches
(31.75 centimeters). The mask
dates from the sixteenth
century BC.

The high population density of the era is evident in the number of Mycenaean remains that have been discovered in many modern Greek towns. Mycenae was perhaps the mightiest, but surely not the only center of the Mycenaean world. Royal fortresses and palaces of similar or even greater size were built in Tiryns, Asine, Pylos, Athens, Thebes, and Iolkos.

Mycenae's mighty walls were surpassed in the height and size of their stone blocks only by those of the fortress of Tiryns, built in three stages after 1450 BC. Its most striking features are the covered corridors and casements enclosing the impressive galleries. Palace buildings have also been found here, including a megaron. The best understanding of a Mycenaean palace might well be obtained from Nestor's palace in Pylos. Nowhere has a floor plan been better preserved. This is due to the fact that the site of the city of Pylos was only built on once.

213

Mycenaean terra-cotta
statuette from the necropolis
near the fortress of Tiryns,
possibly depicting a goddess
or worshiper

Many of the other ancient sites were repeatedly used, new cities built on top of the remains of older settlements. Nestor's palace, comprised of several buildings, was not protected by massive surrounding walls, but it was probably guarded by fortresses along the coast. The middle structure, in megaron or rectangular style, was the actual residence. Despite their differences, Mycenae, Tiryns, Pylos, and the other palaces of the era have much in common in terms of both their architecture and the objects discovered in them. Among their major finds are inscribed clay tablets, most of which come from Pylos.

The clay tablets were found in or near the palaces. The destruction of the palaces by fire in approximately 1200 BC actually preserved the tablets by baking them. They turned out to be of an administrative nature, listing goods, palace personnel, and other details of housekeeping. Both the contents and the time frame of these texts are limited. They provide a snapshot of the palace administration just before it was destroyed. In addition, the tablets reveal information about Mycenaean social life through the many names and categories they list. These texts enable us to speak with greater certainty about the organization of Mycenaean society, whereas we can only offer hypotheses about Minoan Crete.

The Mycenaean world shows surprising unity in its social, religious, and linguistic aspects, despite its loose political organization. The *wanax* (king) headed the political and social organization. Under him was the *lawagetas* (people's leader), possibly the army commander. Then there were the *telestai,* thought to be religious magistrates or landowners. The *basileus* was a local subordinate chief. The *demos* was the group of freemen. All of these were connected. Each class had its own kind of landownership or tenancy. Ownership and use of the land, labor (performed by large numbers of slaves in workshops in the palace proper), and manufacture were apparently monitored closely in the palace. The tablets mention the production, processing, and distribution of agricultural produce, highly skilled crafts for the making of luxury items, carpentry and shipbuilding, metalwork (particularly weapon making), and large-scale textile manufacturing.

The Mycenaeans displayed an urge for expansion. They subjugated Knossos and an undetermined part of Minoan Crete. Their influence reached to all corners of their world: Asia Minor, Syria, Egypt, southern Italy, and the Mediterranean islands of Crete, Sicily, Cyprus, and Sardinia. The large quan-

tity of Mycenaean earthenware found in all these places—more than any earlier type of pottery from the Aegean era—bears witness to the strong increase in Mycenaean trading.

The Decline

Over the thirteenth century, there was significant construction in Mycenaean territory. Many new buildings were erected and the fortresses of Tiryns, Mycenae, and Athens were expanded and reinforced. Even in Pylos, where there were no walls, the palace was modified to make it less open. Storerooms everywhere were enlarged and measures were taken to secure supplies of drinking water. Simultaneously, in central Greece, a gigantic fortress was erected near Gla, located on the edge of Lake Kopaïs in Boeotia. This fortress, with walls two miles (3.2 kilometers) long, covers a total area of fifty acres

Head of a Mycenaean warrior wearing a helmet made of wild boar's teeth, as described in Homer's *Iliad*

(202 square kilometers). In contrast, the city walls of Mycenae are slightly over half a mile (0.8 kilometers) long and encircling seven and a half acres (3 hectares). The fortress at Gla can only have been intended as a central refuge for the entire surrounding area during a time when Mycenaeans all over Greece were apparently feeling a threat of invasion.

The clay tablets of Pylos mention sending sentinels to the coast, drafting soldiers, and hiring rowers. One of the tablets apparently refers to an unprecedented sacrifice of thirteen golden vases and ten people, intended to beg the mercy of the gods in an emergency.

That the threat was not imaginary was proved by the widespread destruction that took place after 1250 BC. This was frequent-

ly explained by the invasion of the Dorians, a tribe from the Balkans and northern Greece.

The Dorians are said to have annihilated the Mycenaean civilization. This hypothesis has a few flaws. There is no demonstrable gap in the archaeological material that would correspond to the arrival of a large group of newcomers. The overall impression is one of continuity after the destruction, undisturbed by any evidence of a new culture. Many of the former settlements were rebuilt and used again, and the existing Mycenaean cultural patterns simply continued. The size of the population, however, dropped dramatically. The society as a whole descended to a lower, less-complex cultural plane. There is evidence of recurring devastation in the course of the twelfth century.

What caused the fall of the palaces and the ensuing decline if it was not the Dorian invaders? The entire eastern Mediterranean area was in ferment over this period. The Mycenaeans were not the only people affected. The Hittites disappeared from Asia Minor and the Egyptians were caught in battle with the Sea Peoples. Possibly these largely unknown enemies of Egypt also swept through the Mycenaean palaces. Possibly there was civil war among the various Mycenaean kingdoms. Natural disasters may have played a role, especially earthquakes. There are signs of earthquake damage at this time. There may have been disaster resulting from epidemics, crop failures, or some economic reason like the cutting off of trade routes, overspecialization, or badly managed taxation. At any rate, the so-called Dark Age dawned in Greece.

Mycenae was besieged and finally destroyed about 468 BC by people from Argos. This time it was not rebuilt.

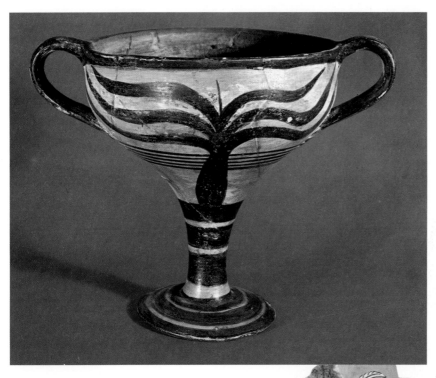

Mycenaean drinking vessel found on Rhodes. Its decoration shows a stylized portrayal of an octopus (1300-1200 BC).

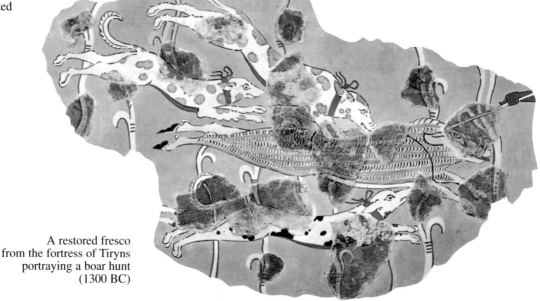

A restored fresco from the fortress of Tiryns portraying a boar hunt (1300 BC)

216

Ziggurat, or temple tower, built by the king of Elam during the thirteenth century BC. On these steplike terraces, characteristic of the Mesopotamian civilization, temples were built.

The Sumerians

The Golden Age and Decline of Mesopotamia's Oldest Civilization

The Greeks named the land between the Euphrates and the Tigris Rivers "Mesopotamia," which literally means the Land Between the Two Rivers. This valley was the birthplace of the ancient civilizations of Sumer, Akkad, Babylonia, and Assyria. The Tigris, 1,150 miles (1,850 kilometers) long, begins in western Asia in two branches. The branches join at Til and flow southeast to unite with the Euphrates at al-Qurnah to form the Shatt al Arab, which flows another 120 miles (193.1 kilometers) to the Persian Gulf. The river begins to rise in March, its many tributaries in the north swelling as the snow melts, especially in the mountains of Turkey. By mid-June it returns to normal level, shallow in many places but generally navigable by at least small boats. The Euphrates originates in the Taurus Moun-

tains of Turkey, formed as well by the joining of two rivers, the Eastern and Western Euphrates. It flows 1,700 miles (2,735.3 kilometers) to the Persian Gulf. Receiving water from the Taurus Mountains, it also starts to rise in March. The floods last until June, increasing the water level by more than twelve feet (3.7 meters). There is virtually no reliable rainfall in southern Mesopotamia, where the land is either marsh or oversalinated land that can't be cultivated. The barren plains the Euphrates flows through today were so rich and well irrigated by ancient Mesopotamians that they were called the Fertile Crescent. Today the main stream of the river is navigable only for some 450 miles (724 kilometers) by small boats. There are references in the Bible to this river (Genesis 15:18; Deuteronomy 1:7, 11:24;

On the right,
a cylinder seal
(approximately 2800 BC)
used by the Mesopotamians
to label property and to
ratify agreements.
On the left, its impression
in plasticine

and Joshua 1:4). The region is identified as the cradle of humanity, its story closely related to the history of the Jewish people recorded in the Bible.

Archaeology

The oldest civilization that emerges in this region is Sumer, not even suspected until the middle of the last century. Work on Assyrian sites (Nineveh, Dur Sharrukin, and Calah) led to the discovery of thousands of clay tablets. The excavations, carried out between AD 1842 and 1854 by archaeologists Paul Émile Botta and Victor Place of France, Hormuzd Rassam of Iraq, and Sir Austen Henry Layard and Sir Henry Creswicke Rawlinson of Britain, were the first of many. Most of the tablets, dating from the first millennium BC, were inscribed in Akkadian cuneiform. Rawlinson and Edward Hincks of Ireland discovered that some were in an unknown language. In 1869, the French archaeologist Jules Oppert first named it Sumerian, because of the frequent mention of the king of Sumer in the inscriptions.

Knowledge of Sumerian history comes largely from inscriptions on clay tablets and archaeological findings since then at Lagash, Nippur, Kish, Adab, Uruk, Eridu, Eshnunna, Jemdet Nasr, Shuruppak, Tell al-Ubaid, Tutub, and Ur. Excavations have been underway for over a century now, but some of the problems are perennial. Because the inhabitants of Lower Mesopotamia did not have natural stone, they had to rely on clay. At first, they made clay bricks and dried them in the sun. Later, they fired them in an oven. The clay eventually fused with any foundation it might have had, leaving only the single compact mass of clay found at many excavations. This is complicated by the

ancient practice of constructing new buildings directly on top of the remains of the old. A refined technique is required to rediscover the original layers. The same thing occurred with entire cities, so that building levels became increasingly higher, forming hills, referred to as *tells*. Many of these tells have been explored but no one has yet been able to reach the remains of the earliest human settlements in the region, later known as Sumer, because the groundwater level has risen in the river valleys. These remains can certainly be assumed to exist. New techniques must be developed to permit excavation at a greater depth.

The deepest layers reached so far have revealed evidence of a people with complex belief systems and social organization, yet used a primitive pictography. These earliest inhabitants arrived about 5000 BC. It is thought that Semitic-speaking people from the deserts of Arabia and Syria began to populate the region. Beginning around 3400 BC, the Sumerian culture can be detected in the archaeological record. The distinction between the two is purely linguistic. Sumerians used a unique language of their own that became the common speech of a new civilization. There were no separate Sumerian or Semite races. The Sumerians became dominant for a time. Intermarrying with the indigenous people, they built a strong and vibrant culture, bound by religion and rich in art and architecture.

The Sumerian City-states

The oldest cities of southern Mesopotamia (ca. 3400-3100 BC) were originally small settlements, usually built around a large sanctuary. This oldest period is called the Uruk period after the city of Uruk. They would become the major Sumerian cities of Ur, Uruk, Nippur, Adab, Eridu, Isin, Kish, Lagash, and Larsa. A typical temple economy prevailed. The god was not only the giver of fertility, but also, through the temple, the owner of the most land and cattle herds. The temple occupied a central position in Sumerian life, not only sociologically, but

Figurine of baked clay,
dating from the
third millennium BC, perhaps
representing a goddess

architecturally. The most conspicuous structure in any village, it was usually built on a number of terraces, forming the typical Mesopotamian temple tower called a *ziggurat*. During the Uruk period, temples were decorated by cone mosaics, clay or stone cones with colored tips hammered into the clay walls, creating colorful patterns.

The highest authority was initially the *ensi*, a kind of governor who officially reigned on behalf of the god. Gradually, the areas that belonged to a city grew larger. The cities became city-states, in conflict with one another. A new political figure emerged, the *lugal* (great man), usually translated as "king." As the cities expanded, they absorbed ever larger numbers. The Sumerian element was eroded even as the power of the Sumerian city-states increased. The Semitic language from this era is called Akkadian, after the city of Akkad, the capital of the first empire in Mesopotamia. In the course of the third millennium, Akkadian became dominant in popular matters, while Sumerian remained the language of religion, jurisprudence, and science in much the same way that Latin was used in Europe during the Middle Ages.

Statuette from Sumer
(approximately 2600 BC)
showing two goats
(the left one is broken) trying
to swim ashore during
a flood

A Sumerian, probably a
priest, indicated by
his nudity and shaved head,
pours water in a vessel
holding a plant, in the presence
of a goddess seated on a
mountain. The Sumerians
believed that all crops
originated from the
mountains.

A view of the Euphrates River, which constituted the borders of Mesopotamia (the land between the two rivers) together with the Tigris

Sumerian Religion

Sumerians were pantheistic, believing in a number of living gods that looked like humans but had superhuman characteristics, including immortality. The most striking feature of their religion is its emphasis on creating. There were four major gods of creation, each responsible for an aspect of the universe. Anu, god of the heavens, had his main temple at the shrine E-anna (the House of Anum) in Uruk. Ki was the goddess of earth. Enlil, the god of air, had his temple, the most important in Sumer, called the E-kur (House-Mountain) at Nippur. He controlled prosperity and adversity and personified the floods that could bring both fertility and destruction. Enki or Ea, in Akkadian, was the god of

Clay plaque
portraying a deity,
perhaps Anu

220

Statue of a praying figure from Umma (ca. 1900 BC), one of the later city-states of Sumer. Around 2500 BC, the dynasty named after this city destroyed its competitor, the city of Lagash. Later Lagash was rebuilt and reached its zenith of power.

the deep waters, especially the deep waters under the earth. His temple was the Apsu, named for Apso, the first waters in the city of Eridu. Enki played an important role in many myths, said to have created the earth and the people from the clay of the Apsu. He was also the god of wisdom and the kind donor of most cultural institutions.

Below these four were the three lesser deities. Nanna, the moon god, was father of the other two: Utu, the sun god, and Inanna, the goddess of heaven, love, procreation, and war. Every city had one of these major gods as its patron and a temple to it where services, including sacrifice, were held daily. There were also gods for farms, for individual tools like plows and axes, for mountains, plains, and (understandably) rivers.

The Sumerians, like many other peoples, had a myth to explain the seasons. It begins with the marriage of the mortal Dumu-zi (identified with the biblical Tammuz) to the goddess Inanna. This was arranged to protect the fertility of both land and people. Dumu-zi, however, fails to please his wife. The goddess, dissatisfied and angry, orders him banished to the underworld for half of every year. This creates the dry season, when nothing can grow. Dumu-zi returns to his wife at the fall equinox, when the length of day and night are equal and the seasons change. His return allows all life on earth to be renewed, to once again be fertile. This was also the time of the new year in Sumerian culture. It was celebrated by a reenactment of the wedding of Dumu-zi and Inanna.

The Script and Its Deciphering
By AD 1900, the existence of the Sumerians had been deduced from the peculiarities of its script. It took almost the entire nineteenth century to decipher it and many Sumerian texts are still difficult to read. The close affinity between Akkadian and later languages does not apply to Sumerian, which has no descendants.

From the time it first appears, the Sumerian language and the cuneiform script were universally adopted. This new writing system appears to have developed out of a number of different recording systems that had evolved in southern Mesopotamia and southwestern Iran. It would become the

221

basic form of written communication in Asia Minor for the next two thousand years. The script is called *cuneiform* (wedge-shaped) because it was written by pressing a pointed stick, or stylus, into a tablet of soft clay, leaving an impression in the shape of a wedge. The clay tablets were dried in the sun or fired and could last for thousands of years.

Cuneiform script started out as pictography, with each sign representing an idea or object. Eventually, these pictorial signs became more and more sketchy, and sometimes changed into phonetic symbols. Thus, the symbol * (a

Cuneiform script is the oldest-known form of writing. It was invented in approximately 3300 BC by the Sumerians. Syllables are rendered with wedgelike characters that were pressed in the soft clay with a sharp tool, after which the clay tablets were often baked. This clay tablet was found with its original clay "envelope" and contains a legal text.

star) was also the symbol for god; both were called *dinger*. The same sign was used for An, which means heaven or the god Anu. In the next phase, * also became the representation of the syllable *an*, even in words that had nothing to do with god, star, or heaven. Cuneiform script became even more complicated when it was adopted by the Akkadians. Their words for god and heaven sounded like *ilum* and *shamû*. So they also read the star symbol as *il* or *sham*. As a result, one symbol could have several interpretations.

Conquerors and Pious Priest-kings
Even though many historical texts from Mesopotamia can now be read, accuracy is limited by the mixing of legend with history. The texts do provide information about inter-state wars, defenses built around the cities, and the outcome of various battles. Sov-

ereigns have left texts in which they claim to have punished their enemies like a "terrible hurricane." Revenge was often likened to the nets of the hunter: "I, Eannatum, threw the big nets against the men of Umma," a king of Lagash declared.

In the Early Dynastic period, the first period with reliably recorded history, Sumer was divided into several city-states. These tiny *polities* (political organizations) were often at war with one another, usually because of disputes over ownership of water rights and land. Many of the historical rulers of these small polities, such as Enmerkar, Lugal-banda, Gilgamesh, and Dumu-zi, became the subjects of later legends that probably contain a kernel of truth. The rulers of Early Dynastic Sumer oversaw a great flowering of the arts and architecture.

One of the most spectacular archaeological discoveries from Early Dynastic Sumer is the Royal Cemetery at Ur, excavated by the British archaeologist Sir Leonard Woolley (AD 1880-1960). This cemetery contained hundreds of burials, dating between 2600 and 2400 BC, most of which included the personal possessions of the deceased. Seventeen of the graves were much more elaborate and were called "Royal Tombs" by Woolley. These burials held rich objects and jewelry, furniture, musical instruments, carts and draft animals, and even servants who were sacrificed to accompany the tomb owner into the afterlife. Seventy-four royal attendants, all magnificently adorned, were found in one remarkable tomb.

Inter-city-state battles ensued. Eannatum of Lagash managed a brief takeover of Sumer about 2425 BC. The last of his successors was the remarkable social reformer-king Uruinimgina (or Urukagina) who flourished about 2365 BC. According to cuneiform records, he was a religious ruler who reinstated many temple privileges. He had a new attitude toward his fellow man, reducing the influence of bureaucrats and forgiving the debts of small farmers. Unlike him, Lugal-zaggisi, the governor of the neighboring city-state of Umma about 2370 to 2347 BC, was a confirmed warrior. He eventually succeeded in destroying the kingdom of Lagash. A lament by Urukagina for his ravaged country has been preserved. It contains a fierce accusation against Nisiba, the goddess of Umma. For the next twenty years, Lugalzaggisi reigned as the strongest ruler in southern Mesopotamia. He established regular trade relations with the coastal regions of the Mediterranean. A new era was about to begin, when the development of a united Sumerian state was interrupted by the rise of the Akkadians.

Akkad and the Sumerian Renaissance

The First Mesopotamian Empire and the Last Flowering of the Sumerians

Terra-cotta plaque, depicting a goddess of Sumerian origin, holding a scepter of snakes. Later this goddess was included in the Semitic pantheon.

The dominance of the Sumerians in Mesopotamia was lost in a flurry of internal city-state battles by the twenty-fourth century, leaving them little resistance to outside invasion. Uruinimgina, the last ruler of the city-state Lagash, was forced to yield to Lugalzaggisi of neighboring Umma about 2350 BC. He reigned over much of southern Mesopotamia for the next twenty years, well on his way to forging full Sumerian control. His plans, however, were at odds with those of the Akkadian Sargon, already ruling the far north of Sumer.

There was a legend about Sargon that said he had been abandoned as a child by his mother, a temple girl in the service of Ishtar (the Akkadian goddess also identified with Inanna). The future king was placed in a basket and carried down the Euphrates River. He was found by a gardener named Aggi from Kish. In that city, he came to the king's court, where he became a royal cupbearer. With the help of Ishtar, so the story goes, Sargon managed to free himself from the king of Kish and to found a new city, Akkad.

This legend is quite similar to others that resonate in history: Moses in his pitch-covered basket in the Nile, and the twins Romulus and Remus, the founders of Rome discovered near the Tiber and reared by a shepherd. It is a legend that suits the founders of new cities and new dynasties, men of unknown origin who perform outstanding deeds under the auspices of the gods.

War between Sargon and Lugalzaggisi was inevitable. There is a list of thirty-four battles between the two kings in the texts

223

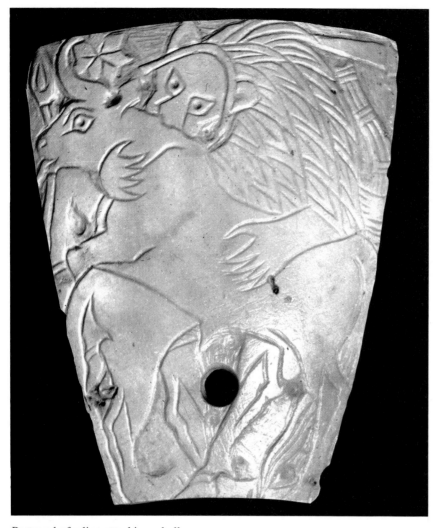

Portrayal of a lion attacking a bull,
incised on a plaque made from a large shell (Mesopotamian, Sumerian,
and Early Dynastic period)

that have been recovered. Sargon eventually triumphed, going on to conquer the rest of the country. He established a new capital, Akkad (or Agade) and the new empire of Sumer and Akkad in about 2335 BC. Called Sargon the Great, he would make Akkad the greatest city in Mesopotamia by the end of his reign in 2279 BC. His Akkadians and the people of northern Sumer would gradually merge into a new highly advanced civilization. It would leave its mark on the course of Mesopotamian culture for almost two thousand years. Ruled by his dynasty alone, the empire lasted only to the end of the century, but its culture and its impact were extraordinary.

Strongly expansionist, Sargon was not initially strongly based. His newly erected capital had none of the prestige of Sumer's ancient holy cities. Using his army, he expanded his economic power. Because he needed to procure most raw materials from outside Mesopotamia, he established a state monopoly over the supply routes for them. He took control of the upper Euphrates River and conquered a number of cities, including Mari in the northwest. He made trade in tin, essential to the manufacture of bronze, a state monopoly.

Sargon initiated one of the most splendid eras of Mesopotamian culture: the Akkadian period. This process took place without notable sociological conflict, largely because the Akkadian ascent to power was never accompanied by the destruction of Sumerian cities or sanctuaries. The Akkadians assimi-

Image of a religious
ceremony at the end of the
third millennium BC.
While two priests
are advancing, two others
play a large drum or
gong. Above them hovers
a deity.

lated the Sumerian culture without giving up their own identity, a phenomenon almost unique in human history. The Semitic language now developed a written form, known today as Akkadian cuneiform, similar to the earlier Sumerian writing. Although the city that gave the era its name has never been discovered, there are many archaeological finds from the Akkadian period. They include a great many cylinder seals of exceptional quality and a smaller number of steles. In contrast to the Sumerian artists, mainly concerned with portraying the eternal and the divine, the Akkadians expressed more human qualities and the portrayal of historical events. Their art tells a story and reflects the change in culture. It shows dynamic movement and is, to a great extent, true to nature. On the victory stele of King Naram-Sin, we see the king storming the mountains and the defeated Lulubeans falling down them.

The major political difference from the preceding Sumerian period was, of course, the establishment of a unified government, the empire of Sumer and Akkad. Although the Sumerian kings had been moving in that direction for centuries, none had achieved the dominance of Sargon. Instead of several more or less equal sovereigns vying for power, there was now a government structured like a pyramid, with the omnipotent king at its head. Sargon gave numerous relatives and friends high positions. It is significant that the old title *ensi* was now used to mean "deputy of the King" rather than "representative of god." He appointed so-called citizens of Akkad everywhere.

Sargon also handed out land under loan agreements with himself as the only landlord. All this was completely different from the customs of the Sumerian city-states, where the gods, through the temples, were the major landowners. Sargon took great pains to justify his political and religious innovations on a theological level. He did this through the agency of the Akkadian goddess Ishtar, who was elevated from the goddess of war to the goddess of love and fertility and identified with the Sumerian goddess Inanna. This religious fusion was largely the work of Sargon's daughter, Enheduama, priestess of Nanna, the moon god. She was apparently a great theologian and poet.

Sculpture of a goat in gold, silver, lapis lazuli, and shell on its hind legs before a golden tree. Sumerian and Early Dynastic period, Royal Cemetery at Ur, ca. 2500 BC

Diorite statue
of King Gudea of Lagash,
ca. 2100 BC

The Lord of the Four Quarters: Naram-Sin (2254–2218 BC)

The old Sumerian cities did not accept all these innovations without resistance. When Sargon's youthful grandson, Naram-Sin, ascended the throne about 2254 BC, they staged a massive rebellion. Naram-Sin not only managed to subdue it, he began to establish garrisons in the far corners of his empire, including Susa in Elam, to the east of Mesopotamia, and Ashur in the north. Reigning over all of Mesopotamia, he extended his power to the surrounding regions. He called himself "the King of the Four Quarters," a title assumed by later Mesopotamian kings to indicate their claim to a world empire. He had himself portrayed wearing horned headgear, a sign of divinity. He wrote a cuneiform pictogram in front of his name, which indicated that the combination of characters after it formed the name of a god. He even called himself the husband of Ishtar.

Such deification of a king was not customary in Mesopotamia (in contrast, for example, with pharaonic Egypt), and it did not last. By the reign of the Babylonian Hammurabi in the eighteenth century BC, the king again presents himself as the first and most important servant of the deity and no longer as a deity himself.

The last king of the Akkad Dynasty, Sharkalisharri (ca. 2217–2193), must have been beleaguered to a considerable extent. He is known to have conducted campaigns against the Amorites, who were from Syria, and against the Gutians in the east. In the south, Uruk almost succeeded in gaining its independence.

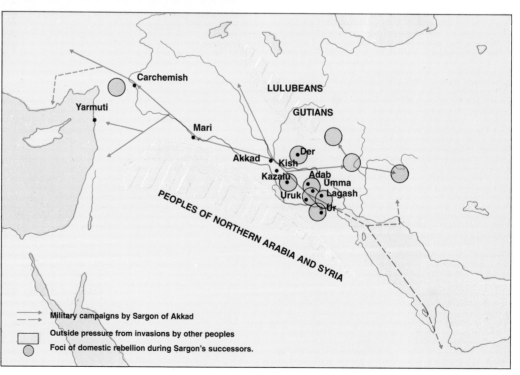

The Akkadian Empire between 2334 and 2158 BC, showing in pink and green the factors that caused the dissolution of the empire of Akkad

→ Military campaigns by Sargon of Akkad

▭ Outside pressure from invasions by other peoples

● Foci of domestic rebellion during Sargon's successors.

The Gutian Period

The end of Sargon's empire hastened an invasion by the Gutians, one of the many mountain peoples on the Zagros Mountains. From those regions, people continued to descend into the river valleys to plunder the riches of the cities. These invaders were given different names, depending on the tribe that was dominant in the mountains at the time.

The Gutians did not found their own empire and occupied only a few remote regions. Later legends tell us they destroyed the capital of Akkad. It has remained undiscovered to the present day.

They pillaged all of the Akkadian Empire. An interesting lamentation, spoken by the goddess Inanna-Ishtar, has been found. It attributes the destruction of Akkad to the vengeful god Enlil of Nippur, said to have called on the Gutians to punish Sargon's dynasty for its conceit.

The Sumerian Renaissance, or the Neo-Sumerian Period

Following the disruptions caused by the Gutians, the city-state of Lagash gained increasing importance in the southern region of Sumer. The final flowering of the old civilization is usually called the Ur III period, after one of its major dynasties, the third Ur Dynasty. At the end of the Akkadian era, the southern part of Sumer, and the city of Uruk in particular, had succeeded in gaining a measure of independence. During the Gutian interregnum, in the twenty-second century BC, the city-state of Lagash was paramount in the south. Somewhat later, Ur became the leading city of Sumer, under the dynasty mentioned above. Under the rule of Gudea (ca. 2100 BC), a Sumerian renaissance began. Splendid statues and royal monuments with his likeness have been recovered. He was known as a good administrator, ruling in accordance with the old Sumerian traditions. The fact that he assumed the title of *ensi* of Lagash, governor in the name of the god of Lagash, is indicative of his piety. While his rule did not differ greatly from that of his Akkadian predecessors, its style appears thoroughly Sumerian.

It is impossible to determine the extent to which Gudea's subjects still actually spoke Sumerian. There may have been Sumerian-speaking enclaves in the empire, but the fusion of Sumerians with Akkadians was by then complete.

Gudea considered himself the servant of his god (and not, like the Akkadian Naram-Sin, a deity in human form). This is demonstrated by a hymn written when the temple Eninnu was constructed at Girsu, the city of

Stele of Naram-Sin (2254-2218 BC), the grandson of Sargon I and, after him, the greatest king of the Akkad Dynasty. Here the king is shown wearing the horned crown of the gods, while defeating the Lulubeans, a mountain people from the northeast.

royal residence. Gudea's building hymn, written on two clay cylinders, is the longest Sumerian text known. The hymn describes years of continuous drought. The crops wither in the fields and the mountain streams disappear. Gudea realizes that famine is imminent and is worried. As the emergency reaches its peak, he has a dream in which the local god Ningirsu appears. Gudea reverent-

Gudea obeys, but in order to better understand the dream, he visits a temple and offers sacrifices. While he is deep in prayer before her statue, the goddess Nanshe appears and explains the dream in detail. She says that Gudea needs to make more offerings and that the god Ningirsu will then provide him details on the temple. Gudea places valuable objects at the foot of the statue and lies down before it to wait for instructions. Ningirsu approaches him. Gudea gets up, and they speak to each other as friends. The god tells him the dimensions of the rooms in the temple and explains the way it must be con-

Fragment of a memorial for Sargon of Akkad (2284-2279 BC) showing a king's soldier leading prisoners

ly addresses him as "my King." Ningirsu tells Gudea, "In my city (Girsu), water does not run through the canals; the water does not shine; the canal does not have water like the Tigris. Therefore, build a temple, the most beautiful on earth and in heaven."

Figure of a bull with a human head made of soapstone. The recesses in this statue were originally inlaid with precious stones and gold. This statue probably dates from the time of Gudea (ca. 2100 BC).

structed. He promises Gudea that after it is completed, water will again run through the canals and the land will again be fertile. The pious king follows this advice to the letter. His laborers work day and night. He dispatches major expeditions to the mountains for pine and cedar and sends others in search of stone. He has copper, gold, silver, marble, and porphyry brought in from the surrounding lands. The tale is similar to Solomon's building of the temple in Jerusalem, except that Gudea lived twelve hundred years before the king.

The building hymn goes on to describe how Gudea himself molds the first clay tile for the temple and holds it high to let it dry in the sun. He places a carrying basket on his head "as if it were the holy crown." Then he envisions the edifice rising, comparing it to a mountain with a cedar growing on a bare hillside. The hymn ends with an extensive description of the inauguration ceremonies of the new temple. These involve many offerings and day-long festivities. Gudea is the central figure, dressed in the ancient cult

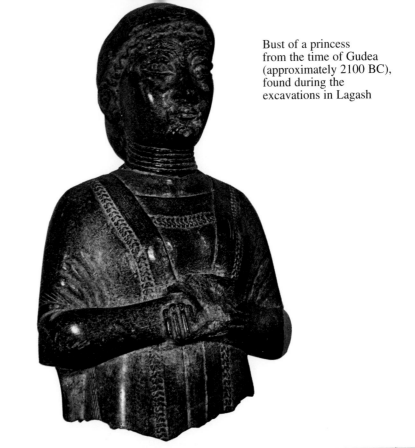

Bust of a princess from the time of Gudea (approximately 2100 BC), found during the excavations in Lagash

Mari, a Kingdom on the Euphrates

Discovered in AD 1933, Mari apparently had two eras of greatness, one in the first half of the third millennium BC and another in the early part of the second millennium BC. The finds from the earlier period were sensational. A palace, a ziggurat, and a series of small temples, most of them devoted to Semitic gods and goddesses, date from this

The large gate to the palace in Mari, dating from the beginning of the second millennium BC

period. The temples to Ishtar and Dagan are especially noteworthy. Numerous statues of Mari's kings were found in the sanctuary at Dagan. Their style shows a strong Sumerian influence, so there must have been close contact with the southern part of Mesopotamia.

That Mari was located at the point where the trade routes from Syria and Iran crossed the Euphrates accounts for its unusual wealth. Babylon, slightly to the south of Mari, held a similar position during the second millennium BC.

The first Golden Age of Mari ended when the city was conquered by Sargon of Akkad. In subsequent centuries, Mari was first made part of Akkad, then of Ur, and finally of the emerging Ashur. It then had a short period of independence under its own dynasty, with Zimrilim (1779–1757 BC) as its most famous king. His palace, most of which was constructed before his reign, measured 600

by 410 feet (183 by 125 meters). It is a magnificent structure that must have been the envy of kings in other cities, even in Syria. Over 300 of its rooms have been excavated so far. There appears to have been only one entrance: a gate on the north side, which led through two inner courtyards to a spacious square, 160 by 110 feet (48.8 by 33.5 meters). On the south side was the great reception hall. A large temple bordered another square to the west of the throne room. The palace also has residential rooms, offices, archives, storerooms, a bath, and a school for civil servants. Its most striking contents are its murals. The murals are found mainly in the great reception hall. Among them is one depicting Zimrilim himself, being anointed as king by the goddess Ishtar, the so-called investiture scene.

The Mari palace was destroyed by Hammurabi about 1757 BC.

Reconstruction drawing of a detail of a wall painting in the reception hall of the royal palace in Mari, portraying a priest making an offering (approximately 1800 BC)

skirt frequently depicted in Sumerian scenes. Finally, the hymn describes how Ningirsu takes possession of the temple "like a hurricane," accompanied by a parade of lesser gods. These include one leading the triumphal chariot, a shepherd, a musician, the inspector of fisheries, and Ningirsu's architect and steward. All these gods are servants to Ningirsu, for whom Gudea built the Eninnu. The extensive retinue probably offers a valid picture of Gudea's own throng of servants and courtiers.

The duodecimal system is sometimes attributed to the Sumerians, but it is undoubtedly older and almost certainly was not invented by one person. The system uses twelve (divisible by six, four, three, and two) rather than ten as a unit. Based on this system, the circle is divided into 360 degrees and the year into twelve months.

Despite the grandeur of his reign, it was not Gudea but Utuhegal, king of Uruk, who won full Sumerian independence from the Gutians. Sumerian literature describes the deciding battle. Utuhegal reigned from about 2119 to 2113 BC.

The Ur III Period

Ur-Nammu, a military leader under Utuhegal, founded the third dynasty of Ur. Reigning between 2112 and 2095 BC, he developed a legal code some three centuries before the more famous one written by Hammurabi. Ur controlled a large part of Mesopotamia. One of the most important kings of the third Ur Dynasty after Ur-nammu (2112–2095 BC) was Shulgi, who ruled for approximately forty years, beginning about 2094 BC. He was noted for his

Lion's head of cast bronze (third millennium BC), found during the Mari excavations

Detail of a decorated box, the "Standard of Ur," from the Royal Cemetery of Ur. Decorated with lapis lazuli, shell, and bitumen, it shows the priest king and a servant, ca. 2500 BC.

232

skill as a soldier and a diplomat. Over his long reign, education flourished. He encouraged the building of new schools and was, evidently, also a patron of literature. Ibbi-Sin, reigning from about 2028 to 2004 BC, was the last of the Ur Dynasty. He and the city-state itself were seized by rival Elam about 2004 BC.

The Amorites

The fall of Ur was, doubtless, a product of the extensive political unrest prevalent at the time. Amorites, Semitic-speaking desert nomads, had been invading Sumer and Akkad from the west for some time. Not all of the Amorites became influential in Mesopotamia. Some were simply absorbed by their new society; others were successfully excluded. One of the kings from the Ur III period is known to have built a wall against these invaders from the steppes. Many Amorites simply lived a nomadic life, roaming the deserts on the edges of the civilized world, often posing a serious threat to city dwellers. Akkadians had little influence in the northern reaches of the Tigris and Euphrates. Later kings, especially the Babylonians, continued this. As use of the Akkadian language grew more widespread, use of Sumerian declined. By about 2000 BC, Sumerian had largely disappeared as a spoken tongue.

Around 2000 BC, several of the Amorites succeeded in founding their own dynasties and taking over major cities in Sumer and Akkad.

One of the earliest and most successful of these was Ishbi-Erra. He had risen to power at the court of the last king of Ur, Ibbi-Sin. Ishbi-Erra conquered the city of Isin and founded a new state in 2017. It remained intact for two hundred years but it did not ever take control over Sumer and Akkad. The attitude of mutual respect that fostered its success is implicit of the reminder to Zimrilim, king of Mari about 1779 to 1757 BC, that he must not offend his Akkadian minority. Of Amorite origin himself, he is told he must not appear in Mari on a horse, but only on a wooden cart pulled by two donkeys, in accordance with ancient Akkadian custom.

Mari's major rival was the powerful city-state of Larsa. The two fought for dominance over Sumer and Akkad for centuries. A third Amorite dynasty in Mari on the Upper Euphrates reached its peak during the last

Statue of Ur-Ningirsu,
son of Gudea and ruler of
Lagash (ca. 2100 BC)

233

Statue of Ibih-il,
administrator of Mari in the
third millennium BC.
The statue is dedicated to the
goddess Ishtar and was found in
the ruins of the temple
where it was placed
so long ago.

years of Isin and Larsa, as the rise of the best-known Amorite dynasty, Babylon, began.

The Amorite Sumu-abum founded a dynasty in Babylon, making it an independent city-state by 1894 BC. Its greatest leader, Hammurabi, defeated Rim-Sin of Larsa about 1763 BC to become the sole ruler of Sumer and Akkad. Although this put an end to the Sumerian state, its civilization would continue in Babylon.

The Mari Letters

In AD 1933, a French archaeologist, André Parrot, started excavations near Tell Hariri on the Euphrates in central Syria, close to the Iraqi border. In less than a year, the inscriptions he discovered proved that he had found the ancient city of Mari. Its existence had been known from ancient texts, but nobody expected Mari to have been so large and so splendid.

While the ruins of the city have yielded their own important information, the discovery of an archive containing some 25,000 clay tablets may yet offer even more. Called the Mari Letters, they are not yet fully translated from the original cuneiform writing. Those that are provide great detail on the life of people on the central Euphrates around 1800 BC. The script is called *cuneiform* (wedge-shaped) because of the shape of the elements constituting the signs. The clay tablets were dried in the sun or fired. As these did, they could last for thousands of years.

Cuneiform script was widely used all over Mesopotamia, but it was a technique of writing, not a language itself. It was used for writing many different languages in the region. Not all have been deciphered. All undoubtedly began as pictography, with each sign representing an idea. Eventually, these pictorial signs became more and more sketchy and changed into phonetic symbols.

The language used in the Mari Letters indicates that the city inhabitants wrote Akkadian, while the rural population wrote a slightly different Semitic dialect, that of the Amorites. The dynasty that founded Mari was Amorite in origin.

Hammurabi and Gilgamesh

Legislation and Literature in Mesopotamia

Under Utuhegal, the king of Uruk, who reigned from about 2119 to 2113 BC, the Sumerians won a major victory over the rival Gutians, achieving control over much of Mesopotamia. The battle was the subject of later Sumerian literature. The Uruk general Ur-Nammu went on to found the third dynasty of Ur. Reigning from 2112 to 2095 BC, he devised what appears to be the first code of law in Mesopotamia. (His son Shulgi, one of Ur's greatest kings, reigned from 2095 to 2047 BC.)

Some two centuries later, Hammurabi, the sixth king of Babylon's first dynasty (now known as the Old Babylon period), ruling from 1792 to 1750 BC, wrote a collection of his laws and edicts. Today called the Code of Hammurabi, it is the earliest complete legal codification known. Although he claimed that the code was divinely inspired, it has been established that it was rooted in an

ancient Mesopotamian legal tradition dating back to the Sumerians.

The only copy of the Code of Hammurabi, engraved in stone, was found in the winter of AD 1901-1902 by a French archaeological expedition. Excavating the ruins of Susa (southwestern Iran), formerly ancient Elam, the team unearthed three pieces of a block of stone engraved with the laws. The restored stele, carved of black diorite, stands seven feet, four inches (2.2 meters) high. Presently in the Louvre Museum in Paris, it was appar-

Upper portion of the stele of Hammurabi, king of Babylon from 1792 to 1750 BC.
On the right we see the God Shamash, who offers King Hammurabi the marks of office: ring and scepter.

ently stolen from Babylon by a king of Elam named Shutruk-Nahhunte in 1158 BC. The top relief portrays the sun god Shamash (associated with justice) handing Hammurabi a staff and a ring, emblems of his power to administer the law.

Below this are sixteen horizontal columns of cuneiform text; there are twenty-eight on the reverse side. The code begins with a prologue that details some of the various gods and the restoration of the temples to them:

"When Anu the Sublime, king of the Anunaki, and Enlil, the lord of heaven and earth who decides the fate of the land, destined Marduk, the firstborn of Enki, to have the power of Enlil over all humanity, made him the greatest among the Igigi, gave Babylon its exalted name, made her magnificent on earth, and founded for him an everlasting kingdom in it, the foundations of which are as solid as the heaven and the earth, at that moment Anum and Enlil appointed me to promote the well-being of the people, me, Hammurabi, the pious, godfearing ruler! To insure that law would rule in the whole land, to destroy the wicked and the evil so that the strong do not oppress the weak, to rise as the sun above the people and to light the land, Hammurabi, the people's shepherd, the one named by Enlil, that am I."

Hammurabi concludes his preface: "When Marduk charged me to lead the people

Impression of a cylinder seal from the early Akkad period, showing a half bull, half human hero fighting a lion and a human hero fighting a water buffalo. Sheep are in the background.

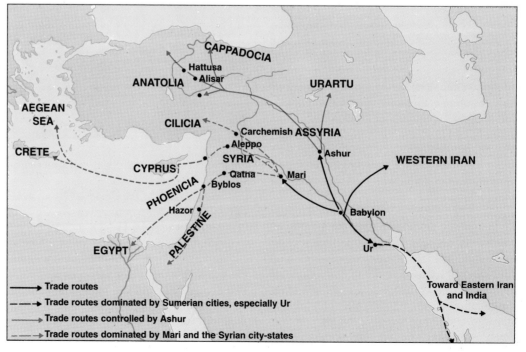

At the time of Hammurabi (eighteenth century BC), Babylon had trade relations with far-flung areas such as Crete, Egypt, and India.

Trade routes

Trade routes dominated by Sumerian cities, especially Ur

Trade routes controlled by Ashur

Trade routes dominated by Mari and the Syrian city-states

236

aright, to govern the land, I established law and justice in the language of the land and thereby furthered the well-being of human-kind. Then I ordered: [the various articles of the law]."

The remark that the laws were promulgated by Hammurabi "in the language of the land" is important. The laws are in Akkadian, the Semitic language then spoken in Mesopotamia, not in Sumerian.

Babylonian Society

The Babylon people who used tablets and the scribe system to correspond with each other may have come from any of the three classes of Babylonian society. People were ranked by law, their rights determined by their status. On top were the free people of the *awilu* class. These were the property owners and the wealthy. They probably lived in two-story brick houses with plastered walls and many rooms. Below them were the free people, the middle class of the *mushkenu*, probably living in smaller, single-story houses of mud brick. At the bottom were slaves, called *wardu*, who must have lived in a variety of quarters. People could

Silver vase on a copper foot, owned by Entemena, ruler of Lagash (around 2400 BC). The engraved drawing represents a god, probably Ningirsu, with the body of an eagle and a lion's head holding prey in his claws.

Terra-cotta plaque showing Ea, god of water and the world below the waters

237

Terra-cotta plaque showing a harp player, a frequent subject of Babylonian art. The Gilgamesh epic was performed by traveling musicians with musical accompaniment.

treated well as a matter of economic common sense, slaves were accorded both protection and certain rights under the law. They were permitted to conduct business, even to borrow money and buy their freedom. The children of free-slave marriages were considered free.

The Laws of Babylon

The laws, written in twenty-eight paragraphs, appear to modify extant common law. The first several, some of which are translated below, provide details on legal procedures and penalties:

1. If a free man accuses another free man and charges him with murder but cannot prove this, the accuser himself will be put to death.

2. If a free man accuses another free man of witchcraft but cannot prove this, the accused will be taken to the Euphrates and thrown into the river. If the river overpowers him and kills him, his property will be given to the accuser. But if the river does not harm the accused, the accuser will be executed, and his property will be given to the man who was unjustly accused.

3. If a free man bears witness in a case and cannot prove his statement, the witness will be executed–if the case involved a matter of life and death.

This is followed by several laws dealing with breaches of contract, property rights, and slaves. Rules regarding buying and selling, exchanges, and expropriations take up most of the code, including the following curious provisions:

21. If a free man makes a hole in a house with intent to steal, he will be executed in front of that hole and be bricked in.

25. If fire breaks out in the house of a free man and a free man enters to extinguish the fire and steals from the inhabitant's possessions, he will be thrown into that fire.

108. If a female wine seller sells not for grain but for money and then gives too small a measure compared to the price of grain, she will, if this fact is proved, be thrown into the water.

109. If outlaws and criminals gather in a wine seller's shop and she does not arrest them and bring them to the king's palace, that wine seller will be executed.

No less than seventy articles in the code deal with family law. The family, although the basic unit of society, began with a contract arranged by the parents. The existence of sons was of great importance. If only daughters were born, a son-in-law would take on all functions of a son. Adoption, rare

change ranks, willingly or not. While the majority of slaves were prisoners of war, some were once-free people made slaves as legal penalty for various infractions of Hammurabi's code. Others had been sold into slavery by their parents. Slaves were considered property to be bought and sold or used to pay debts. Under the code, whole families could be given to a creditor as slaves, but only for three years. Generally

Limestone stele showing a king *(left)* making a drink offering, or libation, to a god sitting on a throne (approximately 2100-1900 BC)

Neo-Hittite stele
from the ninth century BC,
showing a heroic figure,
perhaps Gilgamesh, the hero
of the epic of the
same name

Terra-cotta plaque
(approximately 2000 BC),
showing the demon Humbaba,
who is killed by Gilgamesh
and Enkidu in the
Gilgamesh epic

elsewhere in the Semitic world, was widely accepted. The adopted child could be the child of a concubine, of relatives or friends, or an orphan.

For example:

128. If a free man acquires a woman, but does not fulfill the marriage contract, the marriage shall be void.

129. If the wife of a free man is caught having sexual relations with another man, both shall be bound and cast into the water. However, if the husband wants to save his wife, the king can save (i.e. pardon) the man involved.

130. If a free man ties up a woman who is already engaged to another free man and still a virgin living with her father, and then has sexual relations with her, he will be executed if he is caught. However, the woman shall go free.

131. If a free man accuses his wife of adultery, but she has not been caught in the

Marriage Contracts in Ancient Mesopotamia

Because the Code of Hammurabi is made up of laws dating back to ancient times, the marriage sections describe rules often already in force for centuries. Mesopotamian family law allowed the man to take additional wives, but he was only legally bound to one. On the marriage document, a clay tablet, he listed his conditions for accepting the woman as a wife. It also contained a description of the woman's rights and duties, the amount of money she would receive in case of rejection, and her punishment if she were to be unfaithful.

All this was required for the marriage to be legal. The contract had to be executed in the presence of witnesses, after the bride's parents had consented to the marriage. The tablet was also accompanied by the transfer of money or property from the bridegroom to his future father-in-law. After the marriage was completed, these assets remained in the possession of the bride's father. He had to make a payment, as well, a dowry which remained the property of the wife. If the marriage was not completed through the fault of the groom, the bride's father would keep the money he had received. If the bride or her family prevented the wedding, they had to pay back double the bride price.

Under Sumerian law, the wife could be a witness to contracts; she could own property and use it without her husband's permission. She was entitled only to the income from any assets she received from her husband, but he had to obtain her approval for decisions concerning property acquired during the marriage. The husband was allowed to divorce his wife. In some instances, women had the right to divorce their husbands.

Hammurabi's stele with the engraved legal text. The stele was seized by the Elamites and taken to the city of Sosa, where it was found almost intact many centuries later.

This jewelry belonged to a royal attendant, one of sixty-four young women who were sacrificed in one of the tombs of the Royal Cemetery of Ur. The leaves and flowers are made of hammered gold and the necklaces consist of gold lapis lazuli and carnelian.

members of society, including women, children, and slaves, as the following articles clearly show:

196. If a free man puts out the eye of a nobleman, his own eye shall be put out.

197. If he breaks the leg of another free man, his leg shall be broken.

198. If he puts out the eye of a common man or breaks the leg of a common man, he shall pay one silver mina.

199. If he puts out the eye or breaks the leg of a free-man's slave, he must pay half the slave's value.

215. If a doctor operates on a free man with a bronze lancet and saves his life he shall receive ten shekels of silver.

216. If he saves a common man, the doctor shall receive five shekels of silver.

217. If he saves a free-man's slave, the slave's owner shall pay the doctor two shekels of silver.

218. If a doctor performs a major operation on a free man with a bronze lancet and causes the death of the free man, the doctor's hand shall be cut off.

Next are rules for damages caused by neglect in various trades, followed by fixed rates for services rendered in them. Workers must receive a minimum wage and are entitled to three days off a month. Interest may not exceed 33 percent for private debts, 20 percent for the trades, and 12 1/2 percent for the state or the temples.

The code closes with an epilogue to the glory of Hammurabi, called by the gods to allow "the land to enjoy stable government and good rule." He writes these laws on stone, he states, so "that the strong may not oppress the weak, that justice may be dealt the orphan and the widow. Let any oppressed man who has a cause come into the presence of my statue as king of justice, and have the inscription on my stele read out, and hear my precious words, that my stele may make the case clear to him; may he understand his cause, and may his heart be set at ease!"

The Epic of Gilgamesh

Many centuries after Hammurabi, the Assyrian king Ashurbanipal (669-627 BC) founded a large library in his capital of Nineveh. He had copies made of all the literary and scholarly works that could be found in Mesopotamia. Large parts of Ashurbanipal's library were found in the remains of his palace during the last century. In the past few years, fragments of even older versions of those works have been found. Many of them date from Hammurabi's time, including the *Epic of Gilgamesh*, the best-known work of ancient Mesopotamian literature. We have

act, she will swear by the god and will return to her home.

Although these laws dictate what may be viewed as harsh punishments for crimes that are not very serious, their basis lies in equal retaliation, similar to the Semitic an-eye-for-an-eye concept. There were no laws to do with religion, but the laws display a great sense of social responsibility, protecting all

242

Votive plaque of Ur-Nanshe,
ruler of Lagash, ca. 2480 BC.
On the left, the king helps
to build a temple.
On the bottom right, he is
partaking in a festive
meal.

An ivory board game
with chips from the Royal
Cemetery at Ur
(Early Dynastic period,
Sumerian,
ca. 2500 BC)

243

fragments of that epic from the late Assyrian version from Ashurbanipal's library, from the old Babylonian one found translated into Hittite in an archive in Hattusas, and from the original Sumerian version. There are major differences among the Sumerian version of the epic and the later ones. Because the late Assyrian version, in Akkadian, has become the best known, it is the focus here. The Akkadian story has the characteristics of a true heroic epic, while the Sumerian version tends to concentrate on magical and religious elements and is considerably shorter.

Gilgamesh, celebrated in legend, was probably an historic person. One of the first kings of Uruk, he built the city's walls during the peak of his reign, about 2700 to 2650 BC. In the first tablet, he is described as follows:

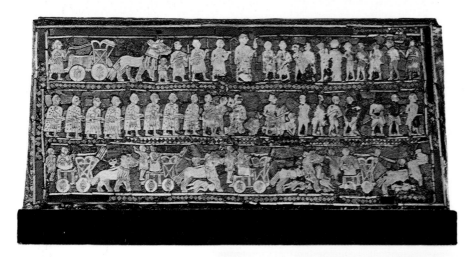

"He who saw everything until the end of the world, knew the universe, observed all that existed and fathomed all secrets, who possessed the wisdom and who went to the heart of everything, who saw the mystery and then revealed that which was hidden.

"He brought tidings from before the flood, undertook a long journey full of toil and sorrow and then inscribed all his struggles on a stone tablet. He ordered the building of the walls of the fortified city of Uruk, of sanctified Eanna, the holy treasury.

"He was eleven feet (3.35 meters) tall, his chest spanned nine hands; two thirds god and one third human; his body was peerless! He strode through the streets of Uruk like a wild ox, sublime of gait; the splendor of his weapons was unmatched! His companions were roused with drums, the men of Uruk were fearful in their rooms because Gilgamesh left no son with his father; by day and by night, he stormed in his anger. He is indeed the ruler of the walled city of Uruk, forceful, strong, shining and clever, is he! Not a girl did Gilgamesh leave with her mother, not a daughter with her father, not a wife with her husband."

Gilgamesh's behavior gives an impression of unbearable tyranny, undoubtedly in

The Royal Standard of Ur, portraying scenes of war and peace. (Royal Cemetery of Ur, Early Dynastic period, Sumerian, ca. 2500 BC)

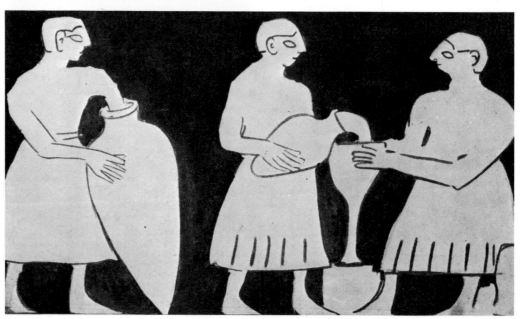

conflict with the age-old laws designed to create a harmonious society. The inhabitants of Uruk complain to the gods about their king. The gods decide to give Gilgamesh an opponent of his own size on whom he can vent his aggression. One of the goddesses then creates Enkidu from the mud. While Gilgamesh is the consummate city-dweller, Enkidu is the simple man of nature, described as follows:

"Rough is he over his whole body, with long hair, woven like a woman's; his hair is as abundant as the crops in the field; he knows nothing of the civilized world; he is clad in a pelt, like the god of the steppes. Together with the gazelles, he feeds on herbs; together with the animals, he presses forward to the drinking spot; together with the animals, he enjoys the water."

This primitive man Enkidu helps the animals against hunters and fishermen. He protects them so well that the people complain to their king. Gilgamesh directs an extensive but unsuccessful hunt for Enkidu. The king then resorts to guile. He has a beautiful courtesan seduce the man of nature, causing him to lose his natural purity. As a result, Enkidu,

too, becomes a man of civilization. When Enkidu is brought before Gilgamesh in Uruk's temple square, they fight each other "like bulls." It soon appears the two are equally matched. Mutual respect turns anger into deep friendship. The two heroes then go forth into the world to perform great deeds. Their first adventure involves a trip to the cedar forests of Lebanon and a victorious struggle against the giant Chumbaba. After their glorious return to Uruk, they become involved in a second dramatic episode with the jealous goddess Ishtar.

Ishtar is an important goddess in Semitic culture. She is the morning star and the goddess of war and love. She was often associated with Inanna, the Sumerian goddess who was seen as the protector of both nature and the kingdom of Uruk. Ishtar has always considered Enkidu, the man of nature, as someone belonging exclusively to herself. Now that he is inseparable from Gilgamesh, Ishtar becomes jealous. She begs for Gilgamesh's love: "Come Gilgamesh, be my husband! Grant me the fruit of your love! Be my husband, and I will be your wife."

Gilgamesh manages to resist her, but he goes too far. He not only rejects the goddess, but dares to ridicule her and confront her

Fragment of the so-called Vulture Stele with Eannatum, ruler of Lagash, marching at the head of his troops, who trample the fallen soldiers of the city-state of Umma

245

with the fate of her earlier lovers, death and humiliation. Of course, the goddess cannot ignore this arrogance. She pours out her heart to the god Anu, her father, begging him to send the dreaded Bull of Heaven down to earth to punish the proud human Gilgamesh and all his kind. Anu grants this request. The bull descends to the river plains, where his roar alone kills hundreds of men.

Reverse of the so-called Vulture Stele, again depicting the victory on pg. 245: the god Ningirsu of Lagash catching the enemies from Umma in a net

Gilgamesh and Enkidu now struggle against the Bull of Heaven. They finally succeed in killing it, and Enkidu cannot resist taking his turn to ridicule the goddess. He throws an upper shank—perhaps a euphemism for the bull's sexual organ—before Ishtar's feet. Pious as ever, they dedicate its heart to the sun god Shamash. Both heroes are jubilantly hailed and welcomed into the city of Uruk.

The Impossibility of Obtaining Eternal Life

After the climactic struggle against the Bull of Heaven, the epic takes a dramatic turn. Enkidu falls ill and dies. Some say that this is Ishtar's revenge. Others think that Ea did not want the deaths of the giant Humbaba and the Bull of Heaven to go unavenged. Enkidu's death has a deep effect on Gilgamesh. Initially, he thinks that his friend is in a deep sleep:

"But Enkidu did not open his eyes; he felt his heart—it beat no more. Then he embraced his friend like a bride. Then he paced about like a lion whose cubs are caught in a pit, or a lion whose cubs have been stolen."

From then on, the story is no longer about the invincible hero Gilgamesh and his glorious deeds, but about the desperate human Gilgamesh in search of immortality and engaged in a bitter fight with death, the only enemy he cannot escape. Gilgamesh starts on a quest for the only human to survive the earlier great flood. This man, called Uta-napishtim in the epic, now possesses eternal life and lives somewhere on an island in the west. (Here, the *Epic of Gilgamesh* obviously relies on another Mesopotamian literary work, the story of the flood as it was told in the Land Between the Two Rivers.)

This journey to the "island of the blessed" is another success for Gilgamesh. After reaching the island, he has a long discussion with Uta-napishtim, who shows him how he can find the herb of life deep in a spring, under the water. Gilgamesh picks the herb and starts on his return journey, accompanied by the ferryman who had brought him there. On the way back, he loses eternal life through a sad mistake. When the two travelers grow tired and go swimming in the lake, Gilgamesh leaves the herb of life on the shore, where it is eaten by a snake. From then on, the snake will be able to renew its life again and again by shedding its skin. Gilgamesh must settle for being a mortal. Although he must accept this inescapable fate, he has one solace: He can point with pride to his life's work. He has built the walls that protect the great city of Uruk. Gilgamesh predicts these walls will withstand eternity. They have, so far.

The epic ends with an epilogue in which Gilgamesh discusses the secrets of life and death with Enkidu's ghost. This conversation does not answer Gilgamesh's tortured questions. This most ancient of literary works raises important questions on problems of life and death. It is both a heroic poem and a philosophical treatise.

Babylon

The Great Amorite Empire in Mesopotamia

Part of the Ishtar gate of Babylon, showing a dragon and a bull

Several different chronological systems for dating ancient Near Eastern history exist. The three major ones are referred to as high, middle, and low. This encyclopedia utilizes the middle chronology, dating the first year of the reign of Hammurabi of Babylon at 1792 BC. (The high and low systems would put it at 1848 or 1728 BC, respectively.)

An unimportant town when its great king Hammurabi came to the throne, Babylon had been occupied by people since before the dawn of recorded history. The first cuneiform documents referring to it occur after 3000 BC. Many others written over the long period of Babylonian influence have been excavated. The city was under the domination of the Mesopotamian city-state Ur in the twenty-first century BC when its founders, the Amorites, invaded Mesopotamia. Around 2000 BC, several Amorites founded their own dynasties and took over major cities in Sumer and Akkad. In similar fashion, the Amorite Sumu-abu founded a dynasty in Babylon, taking over the city from its Akkadian rulers in about 1894 BC.

Both recognition and acceptance of the cultural differences in the population of Babylon are implicit in the words of its king Ammisaduga (1646–1626 BC); he referred to the people of his empire as "Akkadians and Amorites." The predominant cultural influence in Babylon was Sumerian, adopted from the empire of Akkad and Sumer and modified as needed. The resultant culture lasted until the sixth century BC.

The dynasty created by Sumu-abu reached its high point under King Hammurabi (1792–1750). He apparently had undistinguished predecessors and successors who had minimal effect on the course of events. He was essentially an absolute ruler, enjoying legislative and judicial authority as well as executive. A skilled politician, Hammurabi was also a brilliant military strategist. About 1790 BC, King Rim-Sin of Larsa had conquered Isin, a major conquest soon undone by Hammurabi. By 1760, the Babylonians had defeated the kings of Elam, Mari, and Eshnunna, and two kings of northern Mesopotamia, Shamshi-Adad I and Ishme-Dagan. Hammurabi expanded the empire west to the Mediterranean and north into the valleys of the Tigris and the Euphrates. Once his conquests were complete, he took steps to protect his borders.

Despite his victories, Hammurabi discontinued the custom of deifying the king. This tradition had originated in the Akkad period,

Clay model of a
sheep's liver
(approximately 1850 BC),
inscribed with magic
formulas, used by Babylonian
fortune-tellers to predict
the future

He is most famous for the codification of the law he wrote, the Code of Hammurabi, found engraved on a massive stele in 1902. That he was very conscious of his mission, not only to rule justly himself, but to establish a system of just and protective laws, is apparent in the prologue to his code.

Hammurabi attempted to rule according to the standards he set for himself in that prologue. From a central government in the city of Babylon, he cared for his subjects and defended the weak, even among the inhabitants of the two cities he destroyed, Mari and Eshnunna. He treated the people leniently and made sure they were given new housing. He took a personal interest in the affairs of the empire, supervising such matters as irrigation and agriculture, tax collection, and construction of many buildings, particularly temples.

Religion in Mesopotamia

Even though the city of Babylon was the political capital of a large empire for not much more than twenty years, it continued to dominate the culture of Mesopotamia for centuries after Hammurabi. In matters of religion, as well, Babylon surpassed the former theological center of Nippur. The Babylonian temple complex, the Esagila, was higher and more elaborate than the one in Nippur, the sacred Ekur.

In the Old Babylonian period, the first religious and historical texts of any substantial length were written in Akkadian. Yet, until the second century BC, Sumerian remained the official language of religion,

when Naram-Sin had himself acknowledged as a god. All subsequent kings of the Ur III period followed it. Hammurabi, however, realized that there was an unbridgeable gulf between the sublime world of gods and the world of man.

Astronomical clay tablet
from Babylon.
The Babylonian astronomers
read the will of the gods
and future events from the stars.
They drew up long lists
stating their astronomical
observations.

Stele from the middle half ⟩
of the second millennium BC:
the god Shamash on a throne
with the symbol of the
sun in the center at the top.
The deity hands the marks of
honor, a ring and a scepter,
to the figure at the left, a
royal image that was carved
over the original Babylonian
king by Neo-Elamth
(Iran), ruler of the eighth
century BC.

Restored wall
painting from the palace
in Mari
(approximately 1800 BC):
a priest leading a bull
to be sacrificed

almost two thousand years after it was no longer used in Mesopotamia as a spoken language. The Akkadian Empire, which Babylon took over and assimilated, was itself a blend of Sumerian and Akkadian. The Babylon Dynasty, was Amorite in origin.

Fusions of the deities or of gods with mortals were common, typified by the case of war goddess Ishtar with the temple girl Inanna, or the Assyrian national god Ashur with the Sumerian god Enlil. More often, there were changes in focus or emphasis. In Sumerian texts, abstract concepts of the eternal played an important role. This is very different in the Akkadian religion adopted in Babylon. Here, the celestial gods Shamash (the Sun) and Sin (the Moon) appear as the most important of many gods. Two others of particular significance are the grain god Dagan and (H)Adad, the god of fertility, who brings the rain. Shamash plays an especially important role in a number of texts as the great judge. He is the "destroyer of evil," watching over them like a shepherd over his flock. This personal aspect marks a major difference between the Sumerian and Babylonian religious texts. The emphasis on the personal is evident in Babylonian art, as well.

Shamash travels the skies daily in his chariot and sees everything that happens on earth. A hymn to Shamash expresses this:

"Oh, Illuminator of darkness . . .
Destroyer of evil . . . above and below,
Oh, Shamash, Illuminator of darkness,
Destroyer of evil . . . above and below,
Over the mighty mountains . . . of the sea.
All kings delight in Your appearance.
All Igigi delight in You,
They continually hide in Your . . .
In the radiance of Your light, their path is dark.
When You appear over the mountains, You search the earth.
You hold the ends of the world, which are suspended in the middle of the sky.
The peoples of the earth, all of them, You watch over them.
Whatever Ea, the king counselor, wanted to create;

250

This relief originated from the temple of Inanna in Uruk (built around 1415 BC). It depicts Inanna, the goddess of love and fertility, pouring water on the land.

You guard it all.
Those who are endowed with life, You guard with the same care.
You are truly their shepherd, both above and below."

Yet another typically non-Sumerian element of Akkadian, Babylonian, and later Mesopotamian is the "battle of the gods." Here we again encounter the Semitic dynamic, which also left its mark on the fine arts. Life and goodness (the Good, or Creation), described as "that which has been ordered," had to be won from the original chaos. It is precisely from this contest, where chaos is symbolized as the primeval monster Tiamat, that the Babylonian god Marduk gains his great prestige. His victory over Tiamat was commemorated at every celebration of the Babylonian New Year. During the celebration, the creation myth was recited and the great creative feats of Marduk were chanted in the song called *Enuma Elish*. Marduk is also called *Bel* (Lord), a name similar to the *Baal* of the Phoenicians.

Another central aspect of Mesopotamian theology was the relationship between the gods in heaven and their representation on earth, the statues in the temple. These statues were treated, fed, and addressed as if they were living beings.

Belief in omens was important and widespread. Prophecy and prediction were two of the many techniques used to divine the will of the gods. The most important one was astrology. The Babylonians have been justly called the fathers of astronomy and astrology, and the astronomical data they collected is astonishingly precise. Another method consisted of studying the viscera, or internal organs, of sacrificial animals, especially their livers. Clay models of sheep livers with

Impression of an old Babylonian cylinder seal: three lesser gods, guiding a person (perhaps the owner of the seal) to the throne of the god Ea, recognizable by the water flowing from his shoulders

251

A Babylonian clay tablet dating from around 1550 BC, on which an IOU was written

all kinds of inscriptions have been found as far away as Palestine, as have long lists of omens. Details of the appearance of omens were recorded in order to trace their relationship to subsequent events.

Belief in an afterlife existed. The souls of the dead were thought to journey to a netherworld and continue life in much the same fashion as on earth. Because the dead required the same tools, weapons, cooking pots, and jewelry as the living, these were buried with them.

Science in Babylonia

Babylon had a far-reaching reputation as a center for mathematics and science. Calculations were done in the sexagesimal system of numbers inherited from the Sumerians, as were the standardized measures for weight, volume, length, and area. Cuneiform writing had special combinations of signs to represent numbers, with which elaborate calculations, including fractions, could be performed. The number pi was determined by them to be 3 1/8, almost exactly correct.

Surgery was commonly practiced and quite advanced. Penalties for malpractice were detailed in the Code of Hammurabi. Three types of texts provide information on the use of medicine. The first type consists of descriptions and manuals for the interpretation of omens. They run according to the following formulas: "When the exorcist is on his way to the house of a sick person" or "If

The Late Babylonian Empire

The Chaldean chief Nabopolassar proclaimed himself king of Babylonia in 626 BC, as the power of Assyria was fading. Concluding a pact with the Medes from the Iranian plateau, he joined them in attacking Assyria from two sides. In 612, the capital, Nineveh, surrendered, marking the beginning of the Neo-Babylonian Empire.

With the threat of Assyria gone, Egypt began to move into Syria and Palestine. In 605, the crown prince, Nebuchadnezzar II, defeated an Egyptian army near Carchemish

Part of a stele of Marduk-balassu-iqbi, king of Babylon during the second half of the ninth century BC. He succeeded Marduk-zakir-shumi.

252

he sees a snake fall onto the bed of the sick person, the patient will definitely be cured." The second type of text is based on the symptoms: "If the patient exclaims continuously: 'My head! my head!' then it is the hand of a god." "If his eyebrow is white and his tongue as well, then the disease will be a protracted one, but the patient will recover in the end." A third type of text deals with practical remedies.

Factual observation and magical interpretation are inextricably intertwined in the texts. The same applies to the medicines prescribed. First we read about a certain plant being prescribed because of its well-known laxative effect, but then we read texts applying entirely different norms, such as form and color.

Early Babylonian Letters

Much of our knowledge of the daily life of the ancient Babylonians comes from the great quantity of their correspondence that has been preserved. The archives of the palace in Mari have yielded thousands of clay tablets, extremely well preserved by the dry climate. Intended to be read out loud by

on the Euphrates and succeeded his father. He took over Syria, Phoenicia, and Judah, destroyed Jerusalem, and brought Jewish prisoners of war to Babylon. He expanded Babylonian control over most of Mesopotamia during the forty-three years of his reign.

Attempting to rebuild the empire of Hammurabi, he restored old temples and constructed new buildings throughout Babylonia. He reconstructed Babylon, enlarging it and making it far more splendid than it had ever been. After his death in 562 BC, the revival efforts were lost in the vicissitudes of power struggle. Nabonidus, one of his governors, took the throne about 556. Ruling for only three years, he left the city in charge of his son, Belshazzar, and went to the Arabian Desert. He was captured at Sippar by the Persians. Under their king, Cyrus the Great, they entered Babylon without resistance in 539. Persia annexed Babylonia, ending its independence.

Memorial stone
of Marduk-zakir-shumi,
king of Babylon

the scribes, they yield valuable insight into daily life. Here are some examples of this correspondence.

"Tell the boss (may the god Marduk keep him in good health) that Jantin-Erah sends the following message: May the gods Shamash and Marduk give you good health forever. Stay well! The people of the city of Chabur have complained to me about the

Stele from the second millennium BC, portraying a number of animals and monsters. Such images were symbols of gods and are typical of the Kassite period.

following: 'They have given us an order to perform tasks which we are not obliged to do, and they bother us continuously.' That is what they tell me. First they were required to perform these chores, but then the king heard their case, and, since these chores were, in fact, not part of their former duties, they have been exempted from working on the boats. The king then ordered that they should not be bothered again with this kind of task. You have been informed in this matter by people who had too little knowledge about the true state of affairs. Be advised that these people are not to be bothered again, nor may any warrants be issued against them."

Another letter deals with a more domestic problem: "Tell the Lady Zinu: Iddinsin sends the following message: May the gods Shamash and Marduk and Ilabrat keep you in eternal good health at my request! From year to year, the clothes of young men are becoming more and more beautiful here, but you allow my clothes to grow worse every year. In fact, you insisted on making my clothes poorer and more ragged. At a time when wool was being used in our house like bread, you made shabby clothes for me. Adad-iddinam's son, whose father was only a servant of my father, has two sets of new clothes but you are already objecting to one new set for me! And all this notwithstanding the fact that I am your own son and that he was just adopted by his mother. Even so, his mother loves him, while you—you don't love me at all!"

Affairs of state are discussed in this letter from the governor of the city of Terqa to the king of Mari: "Tell my lord: Kibri-Dagan sends the following message: The gods Dagan and Ikrub-el are prospering; the city and province of Terqa are prospering. This is what he dreamed: The god said, 'Do not rebuild this destroyed temple; if the temple is rebuilt, I will cause it to fall into the Euphrates River.' The day the man had this dream, he did not tell anybody about it. The next day, however, he had the same dream. This is what the god said: 'You people of Terqa will not rebuild the temple; if you rebuild it anyway, then I will cause it to fall into the river.' I hereby send my lord a piece of the seam of his coat and a strand of his hair as proof of his sincerity and his reliability. Since that day, the man who had the dream has been ill."

Babylon from Hammurabi to Nebuchadnezzar

Hammurabi's son Samsu-iluna, reigning from about 1749 to 1712 BC, found himself faced with increasingly independent Babylonian cities and the first invasions of

The Tower of Babel (ca. 1887 BC). Many Babylonian kings contributed to the building of a great ziggurat, which can perhaps be identified with the "Tower of Babel" of the Bible. In 689 BC, the Assyrian king Sennacherib destroyed the edifice, yet the tower was completed under King Nebuchadnezzar II (604-562 BC). In 478 BC, the building was permanently destroyed by the Persian king Xerxes.

Upper portion of a kudurru, a type of border marker, of Melishipak, a king of Babylon from the Kassite period (1186-1172 BC)

the Kassites, foreigners perhaps from western Iran. Iluma-ilum began the menacing Sealand Dynasty in southern Babylonia on the Persian Gulf during his reign, as well. Under his successors, Babylonia lost land and prestige to both.

About 1595 BC, the Hittite ruler Mursilis I raided Babylon, seizing Babylonian prisoners and wealth. What happened next in Babylon is shrouded in mystery. It appears that the disorganized Babylon was easy prey for the next invaders, the so-called Sealand Dynasty. They took power for a time, until the Kassite king Agum took over in the mid-sixteenth century, establishing control from the Euphrates to the Zagros Mountains. The Kassites would rule southern and eastern Mesopotamia for the next four and a half centuries, making the city of Babylon the administrative and cultural capital of the country of Babylonia. They fully embraced Babylonian culture.

The city of Babylon was taken from them about 1225 BC by Tukulti-Ninurta I, king of Assyria, but the Kassites clung to the throne

of Babylonia for another seventy years. Shutruk-Nahhunte I, king of Elam, ended their dynasty about 1158 BC, placing his own son in power.

The region around the city of Isin rose in protest, establishing a new royal line called the Second Dynasty of Isin. Under it, Babylon had a brief period of independence. The most famous king was Nebuchadnezzar I, who reigned from about 1125 to 1104 BC. He defeated the Elamites and even attacked the powerful King Tiglath-pileser I of Assyria.

Over the next two centuries, Babylon was ruled by a succession of minor dynasties. The situation was marked by chaos and tribal invasion by the Aramaeans from the west and south. Eventually, they managed to establish themselves permanently in the south, where they became a major part of the population, adopted the native gods, and quickly adapted to the local culture.

From the ninth century until well into the seventh century BC, Babylon was part of the Assyrian Empire, although there were repeated insurrections, with the Aramaean tribes in

Relief of glazed brick portraying a lion. This was part of the Procession Street, which ended at the Ishtar Gate in Babylon during the reign of Nebuchadnezzar II, 604-562 BC. The lion was the symbol of Ishtar.

Fragment of a border marker, or kudurru, from the Kassite period, again showing typical symbolic images

257

the south posing a particular threat. The largest tribe was that of the Caldu, better known as the Chaldeans, long dominant in the region along the Persian Gulf. As Assyrian power began to decline about 625 BC, and the Medes, the Cimmerians, and the Scythians threatened on all sides, a Chaldean named Nabopolassar announced that he was king of Babylonia. In fact, he made himself

The Ishtar Gate from Babylon, now displayed at the Pergamon Museum in Berlin, Germany. The tower was built in 604-562 BC, under King Nebuchadnezzar II, and only rediscovered in AD 1902.

so, reigning from about 626 to 605 BC. His alliance with the Medes and his military prowess brought down the Assyrian Empire.

The City of Babylon

The "gate of God," as the city is called in Babylonian (from *Bab-ilim* or *Babil*), was the center of a fertile agricultural area. It was located at the crossroads of major trade routes, lying on both the main land route connecting the Persian Gulf and the Mediterranean and the Euphrates. Both factors figured in its development. The city was the capital of Babylonia for the second and first millennia BC. It was toward the end of the seventh century BC that the city had its heyday, becoming the center of the Neo-Babylonian Empire which ruled Mesopotamia, Syria, and Palestine for a century.

Babylon's ruins lie just east of the Euphrates River, fifty-six miles (90 kilometers) south of Baghdad, Iraq. Shortly before World War I, between 1899 and 1917, a German archaeological team under Robert Koldewey excavated the levels occupied during the Neo-Babylonian Empire. He found the city divided by the Euphrates, the older section on the west and the newer, including the great ziggurat, on the east. The Babylon of Hammurabi's time is still inaccessible to archaeologists because of the substantial rise in the groundwater level. However, a description of Babylon comes from Herodotus. The original city was a rectangle a mile and a quarter (2 kilometers) long and a mile (1.6 kilometers) wide on the east bank of the Euphrates. In 600 BC, the wall surrounding the entire metropolitan area, including outskirts and suburbs, was ten miles (16 kilometers) long. There were actually two walls, an inner wall twenty-two feet (6.7 meters) wide and an outer wall thirteen feet (4 meters) wide, with a space of twenty-three feet (7 meters) between them. The city had nine major gates in its inner walls. The best known of these is the Ishtar Gate. The Processional Way, so called because a procession was part of the Babylonian New Year's festival, ran through the Ishtar Gate, south to the temples of Ninurta and Gula on the edge of the city. Between the Way and the Euphrates lay the palace stronghold. Esagila, the main temple of patron god Marduk, stood near the city center. Across the river was the ziggurat of Babylon, the Etemenanki or "house of the foundation of heaven and earth." Seven stories high, it might have been the biblical Tower of Babel. Also a noteworthy part of Babylon were the Hanging Gardens. One of the seven wonders of the world, they were built as a gift from Nebuchadnezzar II to his wife, an Iranian princess, so that she wouldn't miss the mountainous landscape of her home. This magnificent city is the city in which the Israelites were brought to Babylon under Nebuchadnezzar II.

Stone relief portraying a group of Assyrian archers. Military operations were a frequent subject on reliefs.

Assyria

A Race of Rulers Founds the First Empire

Assyria, named after its god Ashur, lay north of Babylonia (once Sumer, then Sumer and Akkad) in Mesopotamia, bordered on the east by the Zagros Mountains. It included the valley of the Tigris River. Assyria's earliest history is obscure, although it is known to have been inhabited in Paleolithic times from the discovery of two Neandertal *(Homo sapiens neanderthalensis)* skulls found in the region. Farmers of unknown origin have left their traces from about the ninth millennium BC. They domesticated animals and built houses out of clay, burying their dead among them. They grew wheat and barley. They baked bread in round clay ovens. They spun thread on hand spindles, wove cloth, and made tools, ornaments, and seals out of stone, primarily obsidian. By 7000 BC, the use of pottery was widespread in northern Mesopotamia.

The early history of Assyria is obscure. During the third millennium BC it was under the influence of the Sumero-Akkadian civilizations that dominated southern Mesopotamia. Perhaps due to this influence, at this time the north adopted the Akkadian language and cuneiform script.

It is only with the collapse of the southern

Although the Assyrians seldom depicted religious rituals or stories on reliefs, they did portray winged protective spirits such as these.

Mesopotamian polities around 2000 BC that a truly Assyrian culture emerges in the written and archaeological record of the land of Ashur. During the Old Assyrian period (1940–1720 BC) the city of Ashur was the center of a remarkable trading network. The records of this activity, however, are not found at Ashur, but at the distant site of Kültepe in central Turkey. Giant pottery vessels full of cuneiform texts, written in the Old Assyrian dialect of Akkadian, give details of commerce carried out between Ashur and Kültepe using caravans of donkeys to carry goods, especially metals and textiles. Ten or fifteen Assyrian families controlled this trade, and rich burials in Ashur attest to their great wealth.

Shamshi-Adad I

Around 1810 BC, Shamshi-Adad I, a king of uncertain origin who would rule from about 1813 to 1781, established what was probably the first centrally organized empire in the ancient Middle East. He took over the land from the Zagros to the Mediterranean, including Assyria. Only a generation later, Assyria, under his son Ishme-Dagan I, was forced to yield its control to Babylonia's King Hammurabi. Assyria was made part of the Babylonian Empire about 1760.

Image of an eagle-headed, winged protective spirit

Assyrian glazed pottery bowl, decorated with inlaid motifs in different colors

A courtier on a
fragment of a relief
from the palace
of Ashurnasirpal II in Calah
(Nimrud), from the
ninth century BC

261

Bronze figurine of an Assyrian deity

During the second millennium BC, the Hurrians, a new population group arrived in Mesopotamia. The Hurrians founded large colonies, forerunners of the Mitanni Empire, on the upper reaches of the Euphrates and Tigris Rivers. During a period of migration in Iran, it appears that the Hurrians were in contact with Indo-European peoples, from whom they learned, among other things, the worship of Indo-European deities and the use of the militarily superior horse-drawn chariot.

By about 1500 BC, the Hurrian Mitanni kingdom dominated northern Mesopotamia. It subjugated Assyria, maintaining its control for the next century as the Hittites developed into a rival empire in the north. About 1363, with the Mitanni preoccupied by the Hittites, the Assyrian king Ashur-uballit I successfully attacked them and won back Assyrian freedom. He ruled Assyria until 1328.

Around 1300 BC, under Adad-nirari I (who reigned from 1305 to 1274 BC), the Assyrian army reached the Euphrates. In 1250, King Shalmaneser I (ruling from 1273 to 1244 BC) succeeded in annexing the Mitanni Empire, forming a powerful country. His successor, Tukulti-Ninurta I, went even further and sacked Babylon. Ruling between 1243 and 1207, he was the first to carry out large-scale deportations to ensure peace in the empire.

The military onslaught was seen as justified by Ashur, the god of the land. The Babylonian myth of the battle of the creator god against primal chaos had moved into an earthly context. It was the task of the Assyrians to fight all the enemies of the god Ashur. Statistics on people deported or exterminated were kept as royal inscriptions and, in a few cases, as annual reports to Ashur.

A period of great unrest hit the region about 1200 BC. The Sea Peoples (as they are termed in the Egyptian records) defeated the Hittites in Anatolia, and Aramaeans entered Mesopotamia. Tiglath-pileser I, reigning from about 1114 to 1076, reacted with what might, at best, be termed a preemptive strategy of defense, raiding and razing the villages of the intruders, seizing or massacring anyone who did not flee. Assyria, and indeed the entire region, entered a dark age, one perhaps caused, and certainly worsened, by drought and famine.

By 900 BC, striking changes had taken place. Iron became more commonly used in weapons and the Hittite Empire had disappeared. In the north, the state of Urartu emerged around Lake Van. Mesopotamia and Syria suffered under the attacks of Aramaean tribes, whose centers of power included the area surrounding Damascus and South Babylonia. Assyria, increasingly on

the defensive, had been forced back from the border formed by the Euphrates in the west.

Ashurnasirpal and the Beginning of the Neo-Assyrian Empire

Adad-nirari II (911–891 BC) and Tukulti-Ninurta II (890–884 BC) fought fierce battles against the Aramaeans, regaining the banks of the Euphrates, and initiating a revival of Assyrian power. The real founder of the Neo-Assyrian Empire was Ashurnasirpal II, the son of Tukulti-Ninurta II, who ruled from 883 to 859. He isolated the Aramaean city-states and proceeded to destroy them individually. Effectively attacking the regions on Assyria's immediate borders, he extended the country's rule to the Mediterranean. He avoided the more powerful states, Aram in the west, and, above all, Babylonia in the south. Phoenician coastal cities and small states on the Mediterranean coast paid annual tribute to the king. His victorious armies brought home incredible spoils. He was a pragmatic politician and a ruthless and brilliant general who considered himself the servant of the god Ashur.

In the name of Ashur, he committed the extraordinary atrocities which he reported as follows: "I arrived at the city of Kinabu, the

Portion of a relief from Nineveh with musicians: two are playing a type of lyre and one a cymbal, the fourth one beating a drum. The musicians accompanied the army of Ashurbanipal.

Provincial Assyrian relief from the ninth century BC, showing the goddess Ishtar riding a lion. Here, Ishtar is the goddess of war and portrayed in full armor.

263

fortress of Hulai. I surrounded the city with the main force of my troops. After a wild battle in the field, I took it. I slew 600 of his warriors with my weapons; three thousand prisoners I burned in a great fire; I did not take a single hostage. I captured the king of Hulai alive; I stacked the bodies like towers; the young men and girls I burnt alive. I skinned the king of Hulai alive and hung his skin on the city walls. I demolished and burned the city." There is no reason to doubt the truth of these descriptions. However, such atrocities were not unique to Assyria, but were characteristic of ancient warfare.

The despot proved to be a force for cultural renewal. He restored the city of Nimrud, ancient Calah, at the confluence of the Greater Zab River and the Tigris, making it his capital in place of Ashur. A great many monuments to him have been found in its ruins. He built a large palace there. Tens of thousands

Protective god,
part human and part eagle,
fertilizing flowers with pollen
on an altar, depicted on
a limestone relief

The Assyrian Army

The army, crucial to Assyrian might, conscripted peasants during military campaigns in the Middle Assyrian Empire to aid the core of professional soldiers. It was largely comprised of infantrymen armed with bows and arrows, pikes, and swords; archers were the most important. Troops in the heavy infantry were also equipped with armor. Cavalrymen, riding bareback, carried the same weapons. Initially, the horsemen fought in pairs. While one horseman wielded his bow, the other held his horse's reins and protected him with his shield. At the start of the Neo-Assyrian Empire, a true cavalry was impossible. Saddles and stirrups were not yet in use. Charioteers, riding in teams of three, comprised a professional elite. The armies of Ashurnasirpal II (883–859 BC) and Shalmaneser III (858–824 BC) made extensive use of siege machinery, including bronze-covered battering rams on wheels and wooden siege towers that could be rolled up to the city walls.

Under Tiglath-pileser III (744–727 BC), in

The Assyrians were the inventors of many types of military equipment, including the battering ram. On this relief, the Assyrian army uses a battering ram during an attack on a city.

western Semitic dialect Aramaic was spoken. Over the course of the seventh century, Aramaic began to replace Akkadian as the primary spoken language.

In the course of the Assyrian era, the army became highly specialized, feared, and hated the middle of the eighth century, a new period began. The founder of the Assyrian standing army, he also furthered the development of the cavalry. He created a core of professional warriors (initially only the charioteers, it later included horsemen, as well). The core was constantly augmented by foreign contingents of foot soldiers (archers, lancers, and, later, slingers) from various subjugated lands. The Assyrians dwindled rapidly to a minority of officers and guard troops. By establishing regional garrisons, Tiglath-pileser spread his army across the entire empire. With his appointment of an Assyrian governor for the northern city of Arpad in 740 BC, he began to organize the Assyrian Empire. The common practice of sending entire populations into exile proved to be an effective means of keeping conquered regions in check, but coupled with the use of foreigners in the military, it reduced the native element in the country. Many of these deportees and soldiers were from the western reaches of the Assyrian Empire, where the by the people it conquered. The horsemen evolved into a genuine cavalry. Chariots were replaced by large mobile platforms for the archers to shoot from during a siege. Short and long mail jackets and pointed bronze helmets were standard equipment. Lancers, swordsmen, slingers, and archers were made separate divisions of the infantry. Trench diggers were employed during sieges. Engineers accompanied the army on campaigns to build bridges and other structures.

Soldiers of the Assyrian professional army building a camp. Relief from the palace of Sargon II at Khorsabad, eighth century BC

absolute zenith of Mesopotamian art. The throne room is a continuous pageant of images of royal power. The main figure is the king. Great emphasis is placed in the reliefs on his task as an upholder and protector of fertility, a typical motif in Mesopotamia and the entire ancient world. The royal reliefs are also unique in terms of their style and composition: for the first time, each image portrays a historical event. Yet all these reliefs were created by prisoners of war and forced labor. When the palace was inaugurated in 879 BC, Ashurnasirpal's other side was revealed. More than 17,500 labor-

Detail of an Assyrian relief (eighth century BC), showing inhabitants of a beleaguered city surrendering and asking for mercy

of Aramaeans were forced to labor on this project, the first great monument of the Neo-Assyrian Empire.

Ashurnasirpal's palace is constructed on a modified version of an ancient pattern. It has two complexes of halls, built around two central courtyards, connected by a narrow throne room sixty-five by thirty-three feet (19.8 by 10 meters) long. This double architectural design may reflect Aramaean influence. The same is true of the *shedu,* large statues of protective spirits containing elements of men, eagles, lions, and bulls. Enormous stone sculptures of this kind have been found in northern Syria, but not in Mesopotamia. The blending of Syrian and Assyrian elements is most apparent in the wall reliefs. In Mesopotamia, walls were traditionally painted, but further west, for example in Carchemish, stone wall reliefs were used. A hybrid form was achieved by covering the walls with alabaster slabs and carving reliefs on them, which were then painted in bright colors. They represent the

The so-called black obelisk of King Shalmaneser III, immortalizing the king's heroic deeds. This stone was found in the ruins of Nimrud.

ers, as well as thousands of guests from every part of the empire, were regaled at the king's expense: a total of close to 70,000 people. After the festivities, the king sent the emissaries home.

Shalmaneser III (reigned 858–824 BC)

Shalmaneser III, the son of Ashurnasirpal II, vigorously continued his policies, reigning from 858 to 824. He crossed the Euphrates twenty-five times to do battle against the Aramaeans, conducting thirty-two campaigns in thirty-five years. Not all were successful, especially when his enemies allied against him. Damascus often headed Aramaean alliances, which included Israel. Shalmaneser completed the construction at Nimrud and commissioned the "Bronze Gates of Balawat," reliefs in hammered bronze which once decorated the temple doors at the town of Balawat, northeast of Nimrud.

Tiglath-pileser III (reigned 744–727 BC)

Between 780 and 752 BC, Assyria was ruled by the powerful general Shamshi-Ilu on behalf of incapable kings. Royal power was reasserted by Tiglath-pileser III in 744, the fourth son of one of the weak monarchs. He set out to make the country into an empire. He reorganized the army and the imperial administration. Instead of calling up the farmers every year for a campaign, he created a standing professional army, largely of foreign contingents, with chariots and cavalry as its core. With this new kind of army, Tiglath-pileser embarked on a series of successful campaigns, planning them with the objective of annexation. Following the examples of earlier kings, he deported the people he conquered and resettled them inside Assyria to break their sense of national identity. He ended the menace of Aramaean tribes in the Tigris Valley, subjugated the cities of the Mediterranean coast, and in 740, annexed Damascus and its chief ally, Arpad. After taking that city, Tiglath-pileser refused to appoint a local king as his vassal. Instead, he put Arpad under an Assyrian governor. This policy of annexation differed radically from the one previously used and permitted the creation of a true empire.

The city of Babylon, despite its advanced cultural development, was too weak to defend itself against the attacks of the Aramaeans. Tiglath-pileser defeated the tribes and had himself crowned king of Babylon under the name of Pulu in 729, uniting Assyria and Babylonia under his rule. His decision to abolish tax exemptions for temples and major cities caused much ill will, especially among the priesthood and the aristocracy in Babylonia. His weak successor, Shalmaneser V, who ruled from 727 to 722, spent three years vainly besieging Samaria, the capital of Israel, but did conquer the rest of the country. A revolt in Ashur ended his reign. The role of the new king in the revolt is unclear, as is his origin.

Sargon II (reigned 721–705 BC)

At the beginning of his reign, Sargon II restored the tax exemptions for temples and deported the population of Israel. He was obliged to permit an Aramaean king, Merodach baladan, to occupy the throne of Babylon. He subjugated Urartu once again

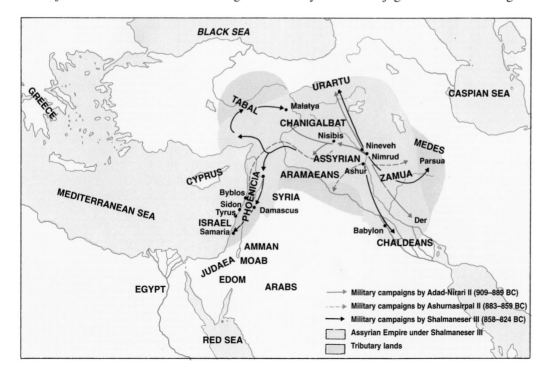

The Assyrian Empire at the time of King Shalmaneser III (858-824 BC)

and took Carchemish. He defeated a coalition of the Syrian and Phoenician cities in 712 BC, annexing numerous states in Syria and southern Anatolia. He campaigned against the Medes on the eastern border and defeated the Aramaeans in the central Tigris Valley and the Chaldeans in the lower Euphrates Valley. In the subjugated regions,

Winged, human-headed bulls and lions, called *alad lammus* or *shedus*, protect the palace of Ashurnasirpal II in Nimrud, known as Calah in ancient times, in northern Iraq.

Sargon built mighty fortresses, which he manned with strong garrisons. Not until 710 did he have time to deal with Merodach baladan, who had imposed such hardships on the Babylonians that they welcomed the Assyrians with relief. Sargon became the first Assyrian to be crowned king of Babylon under his own name.

His empire extended from the border of Egypt to the Zagros Mountains and from the Taurus Mountains to the Persian Gulf. Sargon divided it into some seventy provinces, each headed by a governor responsible directly to

him. In Calah, he created a central administrative organization and delegated some of his own power to his son Sennacherib.

Toward the end of his reign Sargon built a new capital, the famous city of Khorsabad, originally called Dur Sharrukin ("Sargon's Fortress"), eight miles (12.9 kilometers) north of Nineveh. The palace has been the subject of archaeological investigations since AD 1840. Following Sargon's death, work on it ceased, and the archaeologists found the city just as it had been abandoned 2,500 years ago. Sargon's Fortress is more elegant and refined than previous Assyrian building complexes. Its rectangular floor plan covers 25 acres (101.2 square kilometers), and the circumference measures 16,280 ells (1 ell = 45 inches or 1.14 meters), corresponding to the numerical value of the letters in Sargon's name. The entire building is full of symbolism and mystical numerology. Syrian influence can be observed in the style and details, such as the four cedar columns resting on bronze statues at the main entrance. The most important temple of the complex was that of the god Nabu, the Babylonian patron of wisdom and art. The palace was on a somewhat higher level than the other buildings, and its highest point consisted of a beautiful ziggurat covered with colorful glazed tiles. The complex seemed to reach to the skies, creating a bridge to heaven. It was inaugurated in 707 BC with the festive entry of the statues of the gods into the temples. Four years later, it lay abandoned in the desert.

Under Sargon II, Assyria reached the peak of its power. But in 705, during a minor campaign in western Iran, the king was ambushed and slain. His body was left unburied as a prey for vultures. This inglorious death made a deep impression on the world, and his son Sennacherib launched extensive investigations by priests to find out what his father had done to incur the wrath of the gods. Their answer was that the gods had been offended by the construction of the new capital.

The Decline and Fall of Assyria
Sennacherib (704–681 BC)

Sennacherib's first task was to restore order among his rebellious governors. In Babylon,

Relief from the royal palace in Nineveh, ❯ showing King Ashurbanipal (669 to approximately 630 BC) on his royal chariot. Protected against the sun by a parasol, he is surrounded by a group of servants. During Ashurbanipal's reign Assyria reached its greatest expansion.

Merodach baladan again made a bid for power, allying himself with Elam, Assyria's age-old enemy. In 703 BC, Sennacherib succeeded in defeating this coalition. Merodach, however, escaped. Sennacherib had more than 200,000 people deported from southern Mesopotamia and had Babylon's throne occupied by an Assyrian deputy.

When Sennacherib was engaged in the west pursuing a fruitless campaign against Judah, Merodach baladan took advantage of

A row of prisoners taken into exile by Assyrian soldiers. Tiglath-pileser III deported inhabitants of conquered territories on a large scale and replaced the defeated kings with Assyrian officials. Limestone relief dated to the end of the eighth century BC.

his absence to stir Babylon to a renewed rebellion. Not until 689 was Sennacherib able to exercise his power, utterly destroying Babylon. He had the Euphrates River diverted to flood the ruins. The gods of the holy city were taken to Ashur as prisoners. This treatment of Babylon by an Assyrian king was unprecedented, but Sennacherib had had enough of Babylon's eternal rebelliousness. He wanted to break the power of the god Marduk because he himself only recognized Ashur. The battle was also between these gods and between the temple priests of Esagila and Nimrud.

Sennacherib moved his capital, this time from Dur Sharrukin to Nineveh, where he built his palace, giving Assyrian artists free rein in its design. The king had canals and aqueducts built for its splendid parks.

Esarhaddon (reigned 680–669 BC)
When Sennacherib was killed, his son Esarhaddon became king. This succession had been arranged by the Queen Mother Naqia, a princess from western Syria, who for a long time ruled state affairs from behind the scenes. Esarhaddon was a sickly man and feared that his father's murder was the work of the irate Marduk. He therefore had Babylon rebuilt. His greatest military success was the capture of Memphis in 671. Esarhaddon died somewhat unexpectedly on a second expedition to that country in 669.

Ashurbanipal (668–627 BC)
Once again, Queen Mother Naqia arranged the succession, placing her youngest grandson, Ashurbanipal, on the throne. An older brother was made viceroy of Babylon, which immediately resulted in another revolt. In 648 BC, the city was again conquered and destroyed. Ashurbanipal continued his father's Egyptian campaign, going as far south as Thebes. In 650, Ashurbanipal finally succeeded in subjugating the nation of Elam, sacking Susa, its capital. This was Assyria's last great military victory. Thereafter, the empire declined with great rapidity. It is not certain how long Ashurbanipal's reign lasted: The most recent document bearing his name dates from 631. Ashurbanipal was a man of many talents, both a great hunter and a great scientist. He was not only proficient in mathematics, but able to read both Sumerian and Akkadian. Thanks to Ashurbanipal's erudition, large portions of Mesopotamian literature are still available to us. He had collected approximately 25,000 clay tablets in the palace library of Nineveh, and had new copies made of a large number of old texts. Without Ashurbanipal, countless works would have been lost.

His death in 627 BC was followed by a court rebellion. The fall of Assyria was ultimately hastened by the rebellious Babylon, which had formed a powerful alliance with the Medes. The Medes took the city of Ashur in 614. With Babylonian assistance, they captured Nineveh in 612 and razed it to the ground. The Assyrian army fled to Harran, under the last Assyrian king, Ashur-uballit II (reigned 612–609 BC). This defeat marked the end of the Assyrian Empire.

Once again, Babylon had the last word, as it began a renaissance under the kings of the Neo-Babylonian dynasty. This last Mesopotamian period would not end until the rise of the Persians.

TIME LINE

EGYPT POLITICAL HISTORY	EGYPT CULTURAL HISTORY	EVENTS IN THE REST OF THE WORLD
6500 Late Paleolithic occupation in Egypt		
4500-4000 First habitation of the Nile Delta	**4500-4000** Agricultural production allows increase in population and makes for specialization of labor	
4000 Cultural division between Upper and Lower Egypt	**4000** No unification of cultures	
	3100 Introduction of the cylinder seal from Mesopotamia; evolution of hieroglyphs	**3000** Beginning of the Bronze Age in eastern Mediterranean
2920-2649 Archaic period, first two dynasties **2920** The unification of Upper and Lower Egypt under King Menes	**2920-2649** During the Archaic Era, pharaohs were buried in mud-brick tombs dried by the sun	
2649-2150 Old Kingdom; from the third through the sixth dynasties the empire is centralized; various commercial expeditions; cultural zenith in Egypt	**2630-2611** Reign of King Djoser, builder of the first pyramid **2575-2465** During the fourth dynasty, pyramid building reaches its zenith	
		2334-2158 Foundation of the Akkadian Empire in Mesopotamia
2150 Egypt in crisis due to quick succession of kings **2134** End of rule by the kings of Memphis; start of First Intermediate Period **2134-2040** During the ninth and tenth dynasties, Memphis's role is assumed by the kings of Herakleopolis in the north **2134-2040** Eleventh dynasty in Thebes, division between Upper and Lower Egypt	**2150** Due to the decline of the central monarchy, very few pyramids are built **2134-2040** Drought and economic scarcity cause starvation; *Warnings of Ipuwer*	**2100-1900** The Ur III Dynasty rules a large portion of Mesopotamia

Year scale (left margin): 4500, 4400, 4300, 4200, 4100, 4000, 3900, 3800, 3700, 3600, 3500, 3400, 3300, 3200, 3100, 3000, 2900, 2800, 2700, 2600, 2500, 2400, 2300, 2200, 2100, 2000

Prehistory	Antiquity	Middle Ages	Renaissance	Modern History	Contemporary History

EGYPT POLITICAL HISTORY	EGYPT CULTURAL HISTORY	EVENTS IN THE REST OF THE WORLD
BC 2000		
2040-1640 Middle Kingdom; Upper and Lower Egypt are united under Mentuhotpe	**2040-1640** Thebes becomes seat of government of the Middle Kingdom; building of temples throughout the empire	**ca. 2000** Shang dynasty in China
1991-1783 Twelfth Dynasty, beginning with Ammenemes	**1991** *Prophecy of Neferti*	
1962-1878 Political and economic rise of the empire; strengthening and expansion of borders; intensification of international relations	**1975** "Teachings of Ammenemes"	**1900**
1897-1878 Sesostris II		**1900-1700** First Palace period on Crete
1800		**1800** "Mari Letters"
1782-1640 Decline of the royal power under the Thirteenth Dynasty		**1792-1750** "Code of Hammurabi"
1700		
1720-1532 In the Nile Delta, non-Egyptian states led by desert rulers; Hyksos arise	**1720-1532** The Hyksos introduced new ideas, techniques, and gods in Egyptian society	
1600		**1600** Start of the Mycenaean civilization
1650-1532 Second Intermediate period; Egyptian kings of Seventeenth Dynasty in Thebes squeezed between Hyksos and Kush		
1580 Sekenenre leads War of Independence against the desert kings		
1555 Kamose repels the Hyksos to Avaris		
1550 The New Kingdom starts with Ahmose, founder of the Eighteenth Dynasty	**1550** Thebes becomes capital of the New Kingdom; restoration and expansion of existing temples	
1500		
1479-1458 Hatshepsut reigns first as regent and later as "king" of Egypt	**1550-1070** Pharaohs are buried in closed rock tombs with a separate mortuary temple in the Valley of the Kings east of Thebes	**1450** Fall of the palace of Knossos; Mycenaean period on Crete begins
1479-1425 Tuthmosis III; the Egyptian kingdom reaches its greatest size	**1435-1425** Tuthmosis removes Hatshepsut's name from all public buildings	
1450 Rise of new kingdoms in Mesopotamia		
1400		**1400-1300** Construction of the Lion's Gate in Mycenae
1391-1353 Amenhotep III's reign; prosperity in Egypt reaches its zenith	**1391-1353** Refined art and colossal temples funded by agricultural production and Nubian gold	
1353-1335 Pharaoh Amenhotep IV introduces monotheism, takes the name Akhenaten	**1353-1335** Amenhotep IV changes name to Akhenaton and founds the City of Akhetaton, dedicated to the God Aton; "Amarna Letters"	
1333-1323 Under Tutankhamen the old deities are restored		
1319-1307 Horemhab restores order in the kingdom		
1307 Beginning of the Nineteenth Dynasty with Ramses I		
1300		
1306-1290 Seti I manages to hold the empire together despite battling other powers, including the Hittites	**1306-1290** Seti I moves the seat of government to Memphis	
1285 Battle at Qadesh; Ramses II defeated by Hittite army	**1290-1224** Under Ramses II great construction activity, including his own grave, the "Ramesseum"	
1269 Eternal peace concluded between the Hittites and Egypt		**1250** Destruction of Mycenaean society
1224-1214 Threat from the Libyans and the Sea Peoples during Merneptah's reign		
1200		**1200** Destruction of Babylon by the Assyrians
1196 Nineteenth Dynasty destroyed by domestic unrest and short-reigning kings	**1194-1163** Accumulation of wealth at temples contributes to weakening of royal authority	
1196 End of the chaotic era under Sethnakht; beginning of the Twentieth Dynasty		
1174 Ramses III defeats the Libyans		
1100		
1098 Pharaoh's power declines considerably under Ramses XI		**1050** Beginning of the Dark Age in the Greek world
1070 Beginning of the Third Intermediate period	**1070-525** Thebes evolves into the "Divine State of Amon"	
1000		
945-924 Reign of Libyan King Shoshenk I, founder of the Twenty-first Dynasty		
900		
800		
700		**750-700** *Iliad* and *Odyssey* by Homer
672-664 King Nekho is a puppet of the Assyrian Empire on the Egyptian throne		**612** Beginning of the Neo-Babylonian Empire
525 Egypt integrated in the Persian Empire		**586** Fall of Jerusalem; Jewish people in Babylonian exile
400		**ca. 551** Confucius
332 Alexander the Great conquers Egypt		
300		

Prehistory	Antiquity	Middle Ages	Renaissance	Modern History	Contemporary History

272

MINOAN AND MYCENAEAN CIVILIZATION POLITICAL HISTORY	MINOAN AND MYCENAEAN CIVILIZATION CULTURAL HISTORY	EVENTS IN THE REST OF THE WORLD

BC

7000 — **7000** Earliest agricultural settlement near Knossos

3000 — **3000** Beginning of the Bronze Age; rise of various cultures
3000-2000 Early Minoan culture on Crete

2950 Unification of Egypt under Pharaoh Menes
2630 Building of first pyramid in Egypt
2334-2158 Foundation of the Akkadian Empire in Mesopotamia

2000 — **2000** Influx of Greek-speaking peoples on the Greek Peninsula
2000-1600 Middle Minoan period

ca. 2000 Shang Dynasty in China

1950 —

1900 — **1900** Beginning of the First Palace period on Crete
1900-1300 Periods when palaces are built on Crete
1900-1300 Crete maintains strong commercial ties with the Aegean Islands, Asia Minor, Cyprus, Egypt, and the Syrian coast

1900-1450 Through trade, other cultural influences penetrate into Crete
1900-1700 The Minoan palaces of the First Period evolve into centers of administration, art, and industry; first settlements rise around the palaces

1850 —

1800 —

1792-1750 "Code of Hammurabi"

1750 —

1700 — **1700** Internal strife and destructions on Crete and domination of Knossos mark a period of decline followed by the Second Palace period

1700 Linear A script on Crete
1700-1450 The palaces on Crete are decorated with mural paintings; "House of the Frescoes" in Knossos

1700-1600 Mycenae rises to great power and wealth
1650 Cities rise around the new palaces on Crete; the oldest cities in Europe
1600-1450 Late Minoan period

1700-1500 Valuable funerary gifts of gold and silver in Mycenaean graves, proof of contact with Crete especially

1650 —

1600 —

1550 — **1550-1100** Late Helladic/Mycenaean period

1595 Babylon destroyed by the Hittites

1500 —

1450 — **1450** Destruction of second palaces on Crete; the expansion urge of the Mycenaeans brings about the subjugation of Crete, turning Knossos into the island's government center; beginning of the Third Palace period on Crete
1450-1200 International trade by Crete extends to Europe's Golden Age and widest expansion of Mycenaean civilization

1450 Linear B script written in early Greek, used for records in the Mycenaean royal fortresses
1400-1350 Building of the Citadel and the Lion's Gate in Mycenae
1300 Rapid decline of Minoan culture following the destruction of Knossos; building of fortresses and the refuge fortress of Gla on the mainland

1473 Hatshepsut on the Egyptian throne

1400 —

1350 —

1333-23 Tutankhamen is pharaoh of Egypt for a short period

1300 — **1300** Destruction of the palace of Knossos; Mycenaean society threatened

1250 — **1250** The royal fortresses of Mycenaean society are destroyed

1250 Dramatic decline in population; Mycenaean culture becoming less complex

1200 — **1200-1000** Postpalace period on Crete
1200 Mycenaean civilization is repeatedly ravaged by destructions

1200 Fire in the Mycenaean royal fortresses preserved clay tablets containing the palace administration in Linear B

1150 —

1100 —

1050 — **1050** Beginning of the Dark Age

Prehistory	Antiquity	Middle Ages	Renaissance	Modern History	Contemporary History

MESOPOTAMIA POLITICAL HISTORY	MESOPOTAMIA CULTURAL HISTORY	EVENTS IN THE REST OF THE WORLD

BC

5000 Settlement of earliest population between Euphrates and Tigris in southern Mesopotamia

before 4000 Proto-literate culture in southern Mesopotamia; development of cities; monumental architecture

3500-3100 Development of writing; predominance of Sumerian culture

3000 The cities of southern Mesopotamia slowly expand their powers and become city-states

2500 Wars between the various city-states; a Sumerian Empire does not come about

2600-2334 Sumerian Early Dynastic period; cities with elaborate temples, walls, and fortresses

3000 Beginning of the Bronze Age in the eastern Mediterranean

2950 Unification of Egypt under Pharaoh Menes

2630 Construction of the first pyramid

2400 King Urukagina restores temple privileges

2350 Lugalzaggesi of Umma, a brave king, tries to create a unified state

2334-2158 Foundation of the Akkadian Empire

2334-2279 Sargon founds the empire of Sumer and Akkad, a strong imperialist power based on economics; unified empire with a pyramidal structure where the king is the omnipotent ruler

2334-2158 Golden Age of Mesopotamian civilization under the Akkadian Empire

2334 Akkadian, a Semitic language, becomes the written language of the empire

2254 A large-scale rebellion by the Sumerian cities when Naram-Sin ascends the throne; Naram-Sin, "King of the Four Quarters," imposed strict rule on southern Mesopotamia and surrounding areas

2220 Akkad is put on the defensive by, among others, the Gutians from the Zagros Mountains in Iran

2254 Naram-Sin instates deification of the king, but it doesn't continue very long

2160 Gutians destroy Akkad

ca. 2100 Gudea, Ensi of Lagash, rules according to ancient Sumerian tradition

ca. 2100 "Building Hymn of Gudea"; creation of the duodecimal system ascribed to Gudea

2100 Sumerian renaissance under the Ur III Dynasty

2112-2004 Ur III Dynasty rules major part of Mesopotamia

2000 Entry of the Hurrians, a new population group

Prehistory	Antiquity	Middle Ages	Renaissance	Modern History	Contemporary History

	MESOPOTAMIA POLITICAL HISTORY	MESOPOTAMIA CULTURAL HISTORY	EVENTS IN THE REST OF THE WORLD
BC			
2000	**2000-1800** Rise of the new states of Isin, Larsa, and Mari	**2000** Sumerian has disappeared as the spoken language	
1950			
1900	**1900** Peaceful association of the Akkadian and Amorite peoples **1894** Amorite Dynasty of Babylon	**1900** Assimilation of Amorite and Akkadian cultures	**1900** Beginning of the First Palace period on Crete
1850			
1800	**1800** Shamshi-Adad and Isme-Dagan rule northern Mesopotamia **1792-1750** Hammurabi is sixth king of Babylon	**1800** "Mari Letters" provide fascinating look at society on the Euphrates **1792-1750** "Code of Hammurabi" written in Akkadian; "Gilgamesh Epic," a genuine heroic epic and philosophical piece	
1775	**1779-1757** Zimrilim, best-known king of the Mari Dynasty	**1790** Babylon is cultural capital and government and scientific center	
1750	**1757** Destruction of Mari **1757** Hammurabi conquers Mari		
1725			**1720** Desert kings, Hyksos, settle in the Nile Delta
1700			
1675			
1650			
1600			**1600** Rise of the Mycenaean civilization
1595	**1595** Babylon destroyed by the Hittites		
1550			
1500			
1479			**1479** Hatshepsut becomes "king" of Egypt
1450			**1450** Fall of Minoan palaces on Crete; rise of Mycenaean civilization on Crete
1400	**1400-1100** Middle Assyrian period, renewal of Assyria, strong imperialism		**1400-1300** Building of the Citadel and the Lion's Gate in Mycenae
1350			
1333			**1333-1323** Tutankhamen is pharaoh of Egypt
1300	**1300** Assyrian King Adad-nirari I reaches the Euphrates River		**1285** Battle of Qadesh; Egyptian army defeated under command of Ramses II
1250	**1250** Assyrian King Shalmaneser I encroaches upon the Mitanni Empire **1225** Destruction of Babylon by Tukulti-Ninurta I	**1243-1207** Under Tukulti-Ninurta I deportations of population groups take place to impose peace in the empire	
1200	**1200** Fall of the Hittite Empire		**1200** Fire in the Mycenaean fortresses preserves clay tablets
1150			
1100	**1100** Under the second dynasty of Isin, Babylon is independent for a short time		
1050			**1050** Beginning of the Dark Age in the Greek world
1000			

Prehistory	Antiquity	Middle Ages	Renaissance	Modern History	Contemporary History

	MESOPOTAMIA POLITICAL HISTORY	MESOPOTAMIA CULTURAL HISTORY	EVENTS IN THE REST OF THE WORLD

BC

1000
980
960
940
920
900   **900** Restoration of the Assyrian Empire under Adadnirari II and Tukulti-Ninurta II
883-859 Ashurnasirpal II, founder of the Neo-Assyrian Empire, begins expansion to the Mediterranean
880

879 Ashurnasirpal II inaugurated his palace at Nimrud

860   **858-824** Shalmaneser III fights the Aramaeans and consolidates outer borders of the empire

858-824 "Bronze Doors of Balawat"

840

820

800   **800** Babylon becomes part of the Assyrian Empire

780   **ca. 780** General Shamshi-Ili rules on behalf of weak kings

760

750   **744-727** Monarchy restored under Tiglath-pileser III; government reforms; creation of a standing army
740   **743** Attack on the Syrian city-states and their allies
740 Conquest of Arpad by the Assyrians
730   **729** Tiglath-pileser III of Assyria rules Babylon under the name Pulu
720   **722-705** Sargon II defeats coalition of Syrian and Phoenician cities
710   **710** Sargon II, king of Assyria, rules Babylon under his own name
700

750-700 *Iliad* and *Odyssey* by Homer

722-705 Golden Age of the empire under Sargon II; construction of Khorsabad or the "Fortress of Sargon"

689   **689** Babylon completely destroyed by Assyrian king, Sennacherib

680

671 Esarhaddon conquers Egypt

689 Nineveh becomes the new capital of the Assyrian Empire

660

640

631 Ashurbanipal collects 25,000 clay tablets in the palace library

620   **614** Invasion of the Assyrian Empire by the Medes and Chaldeans
612 Nineveh, capital of the Assyrian Empire, falls; beginning of the Neo-Babylonian Empire
600   **605** Under Nebuchadnezzar II the Babylonians conquer Syria, Judah, and Phoenicia
586 Fall of Jerusalem; Jewish people in Babylonian exile
580

612 Babylon becomes the center of the Neo-Babylonian Empire; the city walls measure 10 miles (16.5 kilometers) in length

560

540   **539** Neo-Babylonian Empire conquered by the Persians

525 Egypt annexed by the Persian Empire

520

Prehistory	Antiquity	Middle Ages	Renaissance	Modern History	Contemporary History

Glossary

Ahmose pharaoh ca. 1550 BC; drove the Hyksos from Egypt, conquered their territory in western Asia, and subjugated the Kushites. In Thebes, he renovated the temples of Amon and raised Amon's cult to the most important religion in the empire.

Akhenaton (or Akhenaten) pharaoh from 1364 to 1347 BC. He introduced the monotheistic cult of Aton and built his new residence at Akhetaton.

Akkadian language of the Semitic population during the third millennium BC, named after Akkad, capital of the Akkadian Empire.

Akkadian Empire Semitic rule from ca. 2340 to 2200 BC in northern Mesopotamia (Akkad) and southern Mesopotamia (Sumer). A unified state was formed where, instead of the temples, the kings were the major landowners.

Amarna Letters archive of clay tablets written in Babylonian cuneiform script, found in Akhetaton.

Ammenemes I pharaoh from 1991 to 1962 BC and founder of the twelfth dynasty (1991–1783 BC) during which the Middle Kingdom had its golden age.

Amon (or Amen) originally a local Theban god, he was associated with Re and became the major god of the Egyptian Empire during the New Kingdom.

Amorites Semitic peoples who invaded Mesopotamia from the north and northwest, beginning in ca. 2000 BC, and threatened the cities. They were slowly absorbed into the Mesopotamian population.

Aramaeans Semitic tribes who invaded southern Mesopotamia (Babylonia) from the west and the south beginning in 1100 BC. They slowly assumed the Babylonian culture and constituted a large part of the population.

Archaic period in Egypt from ca. 2900 to ca. 2650 BC in which two dynasties ruled from Memphis. During this era, Egypt was one kingdom, but the division between north and south was maintained.

Ashurbanipal king of the New Assyrian Empire from 669 to after 631 BC. He suppressed an uprising in Babylon and destroyed the city again.

Ashurnasirpal II king of the New Assyrian Empire from 684 to 669 BC. He defeated the Aramaean city-states in southern Mesopotamia and conquered Syrian and Phoenician cities.

Assur Assyrian city-state named after the god Ashur, considered to be the creator and leader of the world.

Assyria land of the city-state of Assur in northern Mesopotamia. Assyria experienced its golden age during the Middle Assyrian period and the New Assyrian Empire.

Aton (or Aten) the Egyptian sun god Re was worshiped in the abstract image of the sun disk Aton. The name and image of Re was the only one kept on the monuments in addition to Aton.

Avaris residence of the Hyksos kings in the eastern Nile Delta.

Babylon city in southern Mesopotamia which constituted a centralist Amorite empire under Hammurabi. Later Babylon continued as the cultural and political capital of southern Mesopotamia. In 1594 BC, Babylon was destroyed by the Hittites. From 612 to 539, Babylon was the capital of the New Babylonian Empire.

basileus Mycenaean official, under the wanax, who ruled a small region. Possibly, he also supervised groups of artisans.

Chaldeans Aramaean tribe located in southern Mesopotamia. During the seventh century BC, the Chaldean chief Nabopolassar, aided by the Medes, brought Assyria down. This was the beginning of the New Babylonian Empire.

chamber tombs Mycenaean graves of an underground chamber and an uncovered access road called *dromos*.

cuneiform a script consisting of characters pressed into clay with the use of styluses. It was used by the Sumerians and the Semites, though created by the native Mesopotamians. It started as images but evolved into a syllabic script.

Cycladian civilization Bronze Age civilization from ca. 3300 to 1000 BC on the Greek Cyclades Islands.

damos free Mycenaean men, peasants, merchants, and artisans. The damos owned communal land. Trade focused on metal and woodworking, shipbuilding, and textile manufacturing. There were also slaves who worked in the palace workshops.

Deir el-Medina place where the laborers working in the Valley of the Kings lived. The *ostraca* (potsherds or pieces of limestone) found here from the time of the Ramesside kings provide insights on Egyptian law, religion, economics, operations at the royal tombs, and daily life.

Egyptian language from the end of prehistory (ca. 1000 BC); the Egyptians did not constitute a cultural unity but did develop a common language. The language is related to the Semitic African and Berber languages.

Egyptian temples sanctuaries for Egyptian gods kept by the pharaoh, who donated land, pastures, cattle, and valuable objects to the temples.

Enki Sumerian god of the deep waters; creator of Earth and man and worshiped as the god of wisdom and culture.

Enlil Sumerian god of Earth and sky, responsible for prosperity and misfortune.

ensi head of the Sumerian city-state; a temple king and ruler of the city on behalf of the deity and the temple. In the Akkadian Empire, *ensis* became deputies ruling on behalf of the king.

Evans, Arthur archaeologist and discoverer of the Minoan civilization. In AD 1900, he started excavating Knossos and reconstructed the palace in Knossos.

First Interregnum period in Egyptian history from ca. 2150 to 2040 BC characterized by a decline of central royalty, economic decline, and starvation.

First Palace period period of the Minoan civilization from 1900 to 1700 BC. There are no palaces left from this period.

Gilgamesh epic epic from Mesopotamian literature which was handed down in different versions from different eras. It describes the life of Gilgamesh, the king of Uruk, who searches for the herb of life together with his friend, Enkidu.

Gla city in Boeotia where a large fortress was built in the thirteenth century BC as a refuge for the local populace.

God State of Amon name for Thebes which evolved during the Third Interregnum when it became a separate state ruled by Amon's high priests.

Gutians Iranian mountain peoples who invaded the Akkadian Empire repeatedly between ca. 2230 and 2100 BC and plundered the cities. Shortly after 2200 they destroyed Akkad.

Hammurabi king of Babylon from 1792 to 1750 BC. He defeated the kings of Larsa and Assur and conquered Mari. He drew up a legal code and abolished the deification of kings.

Hatshepsut regent of Tuthmosis III; ruled from ca. 1484 to 1468 BC as king of Egypt, portrayed as a man. She sent commercial expeditions to, among others, the land of Punt, which was famous for its exotic wares.

Helladic culture Bronze Age culture from ca. 3300 to 1000 BC on the Greek mainland.

Herakleopolis city in northern Egypt where a kingdom was founded by local administrators during the First Interregnum.

Herihor general at the end of the New Kingdom. He was to restore order in Thebes but took power as the high priest of Amon.

hieratic simplified, quicker version of hieroglyphic writing written in ink on papyrus scrolls.

277

hieroglyphs oldest Egyptian script, originally based on images but later, as a result of the need to represent abstract concepts, it developed into a combination of ideograms, syllable signs, and letters.

high priests of Amon the priests in Thebes whose power increased in the New Kingdom due to the increasing wealth of the temples.

Horemheb pharaoh from 1333 to 1306 BC; had administrative and military experience and definitively restored the conditions that existed before the Amarna period.

Horus Egyptian sun god and son of Osiris, represented as a falcon. The pharaohs were considered his incarnation and represented his power on Earth.

Hurrians tribe from the east which settled in northern Mesopotamia beginning ca. 1800 BC. They founded the Mitanni Empire ruled by a militarily superior Indo-European elite. After 1200, the Hurrians settled in Urartu and from there conquered parts of Syria and Phoenicia.

Hyksos Asiatic rulers who settled in the Nile Delta during the Second Interregnum and ruled a large portion of northern Egypt. They were expelled ca. 1550 BC by Ahmose.

Inanna Sumerian fertility goddess, daughter of the god of heaven and ruler of the gods, Anu. She merged with the Semitic Ishtar during the Akkadian Empire and became the goddess of love and fertility.

Ishtar Semitic war goddess. She merged with Inanna into the goddess of love and fertility. Sargon I realized this Sumerian-Semitic mixture to promote the integration of the Sumerian and Semitic civilizations.

Isin Sumerian city-state founded ca. 2000 BC by Isbierra. Until ca. 1800 BC, the city comprised a large empire in southern Mesopotamia in addition to the other powerful city-state of Larsa.

Kamares pottery refined Minoan pottery from the First Palace period, usually manufactured on potter's wheels and decorated with helical and plant designs in light colors on a blue-black background.

Kassites mountain people who invaded Mesopotamia from the east after 1800 BC. They introduced the chariot. From 1600 onward the Kassites ruled Babylon until ca. 1200.

Khamose pharaoh in Thebes at the end of the Second Interregnum. He tried to expel the Hyksos from the north and thwarted their attempts to form an alliance with the Kushites.

Knossos Minoan settlement housing a large palace from the Second Palace period until ca. 1300 BC.

Kush kingdom south of Egypt. In the Late era the Kushites ruled Egypt and were expelled by the Assyrians in 664 BC.

Lagash Sumerian city-state which constituted a dominant empire in southern Mesopotamia during the Gutian Interregnum (twenty-second century BC).

Larsa Sumerian city-state which constituted a powerful kingdom in Sumer next to the empire of Isin during the Sumerian Renaissance between ca. 2000 and 1800 BC.

Late era period in Egyptian history from ca. 730 to 332 BC during which Egypt was ruled by foreign powers: the Kushites, the Assyrians, and the Persians.

Late Mycenaean era period from ca. 1250 to 1000 BC during which the decline of the Mycenaean civilization took place slowly due to invasions by unknown enemies, civil wars, natural disasters, overpopulation, and economic decline.

lawagetas Mycenaean official under the wanax. *Lawagetas* means leader of the people, most probably army commander.

Libyans African tribes that threatened Egypt from the west. They were fought by Sethi but continued to be a threat. In the Third Interregnum they formed kingdoms in the Nile Delta and ended up usurping the pharaoh's power.

Linear A script found on Minoan clay tablets in the palace complexes. Never deciphered, the script is probably a syllabic script and a simplified form of hieroglyphs.

Linear B script found on Mycenaean clay tablets on the Greek mainland and in Knossos. It is a syllabic script based on the characters of Linear A. The language of the Linear B tablets is Greek. It was deciphered in AD 1953.

Lower Egypt northern Egypt comprising the Nile Delta with its flat and fertile land.

lugal political leader (king) in the Sumerian city-states. He assumed the highest position of power from the ensis.

Lugalzaggesi king of the Sumerian city-state of Umma around 2350 BC. He defeated Urukagina of Lagash and destroyed the city. He also conquered Nippur and Uruk.

Maat Egyptian principle of order in the universe. As the son of Amon-Re the pharaoh was to uphold order. He was in charge of fertility and prosperity, and he protected gods and men against enemies and the forces of nature.

Manetho priest who drew up a history of Egypt in the third century BC and divided the pharaohs in dynasties.

Marduk Babylonian sun god. He became god of the state under Hammurabi and was considered the creator of Earth and god of wisdom.

Mari Semitic commercial center on the middle course of the Euphrates. Its first flowering ended with the conquest by Sargon I,

after which Mari was ruled by Akkad, Ur, and Ashur. Between ca. 1780 and 1760 BC, Mari was again independent but was destroyed in ca. 1760.

megaron center of the Mycenaean palace fortresses consisting of an oblong room with a hearth. The megaron also contained a forecourt with a row of columns.

Memphis city in Lower Egypt and residence of the pharaoh during the Old Kingdom and during the time of the Ramesside kings.

Mesopotamia area in the Near East surrounding the Tigris and Euphrates Rivers. Floods and irrigation made the land fertile, and around 4500 BC the first agricultural settlements were founded here.

Middle Assyrian period period in Mesopotamian history from the fourteenth century to ca. 1100 BC in which Assyria grew to become a major power. The kingdom fell into ruin as a result of invasions by the Aramaeans.

Middle Egyptian language of the Middle Kingdom which continued to exist for approximately two thousand years as the written language of literary and religious texts.

Middle Egyptian literature literary texts from the Middle Kingdom characterized by criticism of society and disappointment with tradition and the hereafter.

Middle Kingdom period period in Egyptian history from ca. 2040 to 1640 BC during which unity was restored by the Theban kings. The period was characterized by a flowering of the economy, the arts, and literature.

Minoan ceramics Bronze Age pottery. The Kamares pottery dates from the First Palace period. In the Second Palace period it was decorated with lively plants and marine animals in dark colors on a light background. The motifs were arranged in a more orderly fashion after the Third Palace period.

Minoan cities settlements with an urban character, paved streets, houses, and workshops. They were located near the palaces, but there were also separate cities such as Gournia on eastern Crete.

Minoan civilization Bronze Age civilization on Crete from ca. 3300 to 1000 BC, divided in the period before the palaces (3300–1900 BC), the palace periods (1900–1200 BC), and the period after the palaces (1200–1000 BC).

Minoan frescos colorful murals. Initially the palace walls were decorated with plants, later also with animals, such as birds and fish.

Minoan palaces Cretan building complexes which contained an inner court with storage rooms, living and work chambers, and representative areas during the Second Palace period.

Minoan religion probably consisted of fertility rites, usually in the open air, with processions and dances. Trees, snakes, bulls, and double axes were important elements. There are signs of human sacrifice.

Minoan villas small building complexes built on the same plan as the palaces. Possibly these were seats for officials representing central rule.

Minos legendary king of Crete for whom the Bronze Age Minoan civilization is named. He had the Minotaur, a monster, who was half bull, half man, locked up in the labyrinth. This myth is possibly reminiscent of the Cretan bull cult and the complex palaces.

Mitanni Kingdom Hurrian Kingdom from ca. 1500 to 1350 BC in northern Mesopotamia consisting of the Hurrians under an Indo-European elite. The Mitanni warred with Egypt and concluded an alliance with Tuthmosis III. They dominated Assyria but were assimilated into Assyria in ca. 1350.

Mycenae Bronze Age settlement on the Peloponnisos where a palace fortress was built after 1450 BC. Schliemann discovered its rich royal tombs dating from the sixteenth century BC.

Mycenaean culture last stage of the Helladic civilization, starting in ca. 1600 BC with its golden age from 1400 to 1200. The Mycenaean world was divided into separate kingdoms which did not form one political unit but showed social, religious, and linguistic similarities.

Mycenaean palaces walled palace fortresses, containing the megaron, dwellings, storehouses, and workshops, and their economic function was comparable to that of the Minoan palaces.

Naramsin king of the Akkadian Empire from ca. 2260 to 2230 BC. He suppressed a rebellion by the Sumerian cities and conquered the areas surrounding Mesopotamia. He deified royal power in the Akkadian Empire.

Nebuchadnezzar II king of the New Babylonian Empire from 605 to 562 BC. Together with the Medes, his father had brought down the Assyrian Empire. Nebuchadnezzar conquered Syria, Phoenicia, and Judah. He built Babylon into an impressive capital.

Nekho pharaoh from 609 to 595 BC who threw off the Assyrian yoke. During his successors' reigns, Egypt developed again into an independent state until the Persians conquered Egypt in 525.

New Assyrian Empire Assyrian Empire from ca. 900 to 612 BC that conquered Mesopotamia, Syria, Phoenicia, Palestine, and Egypt (in 671). After Tiglath-pileser III, conquered areas were no longer sacked but annexed, thus creating a worldwide empire. In 612 the empire was brought down by invasions from the Aramaeans in Babylonia and the Medes.

New Babylonian Empire rule by the Chaldeans over Mesopotamia out of Babylon. The empire arose in 612 BC after the fall of the Assyrian Empire and was conquered by the Persians in 539. Syria, Judah, and Phoenicia were annexed.

New Kingdom era era in Egyptian history from ca. 1550 to 1070 BC, when Egypt reached its greatest land area and became prosperous from agriculture, trade, and income from the conquered territories, such as western Asia (Syria-Palestine), Kush, and Nubia. The building of temples and the arts experienced a golden age.

Nile river in Egypt forming a river delta on the Mediterranean Sea. During the annual rainy season in central Africa, the Nile floods its banks, rendering the Nile Valley fertile and suitable for agriculture and horticulture.

Old Babylonian era period in the history of Mesopotamia from ca. 1800 to 1600 BC, when the Amorite (Semitic) culture was dominant in southern Mesopotamia. Babylon was its economic, political, and cultural center.

Old Kingdom period period in Egyptian history from ca. 2650 to 2150 BC, also called the Pyramid period for the large number of pyramids built. The organization of manpower to build these illustrates the power of Egypt's central administration.

Osiris Egyptian god of fertility and ruler of the Kingdom of the Dead. In the First Interregnum the cult of Osiris became popular. The Egyptians could reach the hereafter via Osiris; hence, the pharaoh became less important as a protector.

papyrus writing material made by crisscrossing strips of papyrus reeds. These were shaped into rolls to be written on in ink.

pharaoh Egyptian king portrayed as the incarnation of the falcon god, creator of the world. He was legislator, military general, and religious leader, and protected the Maat. Later he was considered the son of Re and incarnation of Horus. After his death he was deified.

Pylos Mycenaean settlement on the Peloponnisos where a palace fortress was built after 1450 BC. It was not walled, but was probably protected by fortresses along the coast. Pylos was destroyed around 1200. Many Linear B clay tablets were found here.

pyramids Egyptian royal tombs consisting of a stone pyramid which symbolized the original mountain of the creation. An extensive complex of buildings was also part of it. The first pyramid was a step pyramid. The height of pyramid building took place in the fourth dynasty (2600–2460 BC) when the pyramids became larger and had smoother surfaces.

Ramesside kings period in Egyptian history from 1306 to 1070 BC named after the nineteenth and twentieth dynasties when the name of most pharaohs was Ramses.

Ramses II pharaoh from 1290 to 1224 BC. Among his numerous building projects were his own temple, the Ramesseum, and the expansion of the residence in Avaris.

Re (or Ra) Egyptian sun god. His most important temple stood in Heliopolis. The pharaoh was considered his son and ascended to his heavenly empire after death. Re was later associated with Amon.

sarcophagi Egyptian wooden coffins in which the dead were conserved, swathed in linen and buried. Thus, the deceased could join Osiris. The coffin was decorated with magical sayings to simplify access to the Kingdom of the Dead.

Sargon I founder and king of the Akkadian Empire from ca. 2340 to 2290 BC. Sargon based his power on the state monopoly in raw materials, and he was the largest landowner.

Sargon II king of the New Assyrian Kingdom from 722 to 705 BC. He subjugated the Syrian and Phoenician coastal cities, defeated the Hurrians from Urartu, and defeated the Aramaean king Merodach-baladan who had conquered Babylon. He then became the new king of Babylon.

Schliemann, Heinrich amateur archaeologist who conducted excavations after AD 1871 in Troy (Asia Minor) and near Mycenae after 1876. He considered the *Iliad* and *Odyssey* by the eighth-century BC epic poet Homer as historically correct.

seal stones Minoan jewelry which served as a personal seal and amulet. They were decorated with geometric animal and human figures. After 1900 BC they also show hieroglyphic characters, the precursors of the Linear A script.

Sea Peoples groups who threatened the coasts of the eastern Mediterranean, including the Nile Delta, during the time of the Ramesside kings. The Philistines were one of the Sea Peoples.

Second Interregnum period in Egyptian history from ca. 1783 to 1550 BC when central power broke down due to the arrival of foreigners and foreign rulers in Lower Egypt, such as the Hyksos.

Second Palace period flowering era of Minoan civilization from 1700 to 1450 BC. During this time the palaces at Knossos, Phaistos, and Mallia were rebuilt. Intensive trade with the east, Egypt, the Aegean Islands, and the Greek mainland were maintained.

Semites people residing in northern and southern Mesopotamia. They spoke a language different from the Sumerians and were largely rural dwellers. After 2400 BC, they dominated and founded the Akkadian Empire. The Akkadian and Sumerian civilizations rapidly became one.

Sennacherib king of the New Assyrian Kingdom from 705 to 681 BC. He defeated the Aramaean king Merodach-baladan in

703, who again took power in Babylon. When Babylon rebelled again under Merodach-baladan, Sennacherib razed Babylon to the ground in 689. His successor rebuilt the city.

Sesostris III pharaoh from ca. 1880 to 1840 BC. He ended the power and independence of the local administrators and established a centralized system of royal supervisors. He expanded Egypt with territory in Palestine.

Seth Egyptian god of aggression, chaos, and darkness. He killed Osiris whose life was restored by the goddess Isis. He was associated with the Hyksos god Baal.

Sethi I pharaoh from ca. 1302 to 1290 BC. He conquered the Libyans and had temples built, including a temple in Abydos dedicated to the gods and the pharaoh. He built palaces in Memphis and near Avaris.

Sethnakht pharaoh from ca. 1184 to 1182 BC. He ended domestic unrest during the era of the Ramesside kings, caused by internecine fighting for succession of the throne. He became the founder of the twentieth dynasty.

Sumerian language which died out as a spoken language around 2000 BC as the Amorites reinforced the Semitic cultural element in Mesopotamia. It continued as a religious language until the second century BC.

Sumerian Renaissance period in Mesopotamian history from ca. 2200 to ca. 1800 BC when the Sumerian civilization flowered again. Major centers of the Sumerian Renaissance were Lagash, Ur, Isin, and Larsa. Invasions by the Amorite nomads ended the renaissance.

Sumerians people who were settled in southern Mesopotamia (Sumer). They lived in independent city-states dominated by a temple economy. Lugalzaggesi tried to create a Sumerian unified state, but the rise of the Akkadian Empire (ca. 2340 BC) prevented this.

telestai Mycenaean officials under the wanax. They probably performed religious tasks and possibly were landowners.

temple economy Sumerian administrative form where temples owned and operated most of the land and cattle. The highest power was in the hands of so-called ensis. Later the lugal became the highest commander.

Thebes city in Upper Egypt, religious center and residence during the Middle Kingdom and New Kingdom until ca. 1300 BC. From ca. 1070 onward, Thebes became an independent kingdom ruled by the high priests of Amon. In and around Thebes there are many temples and royal tombs in the Valley of the Kings.

Thera volcanic island north of Crete where a Minoan-like civilization existed during the Bronze Age. A volcanic eruption destroyed Thera around 1500 BC. This possibly affected the destruction of the Minoan palaces (ca. 1450 BC).

Third Interregnum period in Egyptian history from ca. 1070 to 730 BC during which Egypt was divided into the pharaoh's territory and the divine state of Amon. Finally the pharaoh's power was usurped by Libyan principalities.

Third Palace period period in the Minoan civilization from 1450 to 1200 BC in which Mycenaeans ruled Crete after a number of palaces were destroyed due to internal fighting, invasions, and earthquakes. Knossos again became the administrative center and trade became more international.

tholos Mycenaean domed grave for the elite occurring after ca. 1600 BC, consisting of a round hole in the ground, covered with a dome of stone blocks covered with soil and flagstones as reinforcement. A grave stone was placed on top.

Tiglath-pileser III king of the New Assyrian Kingdom from 745 to 727 BC. He created a professional army with chariots and cavalry as its center. He defeated the Aramaean and Syrian city-states, annexed their territory, and deported some of the population. He conquered Babylon and was crowned its king.

Tiryns Mycenaean settlement on the Peloponnisos where a palace fortress was built after 1450 BC. Like the other fortresses, it was surrounded by Cyclopean walls consisting of large limestone blocks, containing vaulted galleries.

Tutankhamen pharaoh from ca. 1345 to 1335 BC. He left the residence at Akhetaton and began restoring the chaos and dissatisfaction created by Akhenaton by resuming the cult of deities. His grave was left untouched and contained precious funerary treasures.

Tuthmosis III pharaoh from ca. 1490 to 1438 BC. He ruled together with Hatshepsut who reigned as king from ca. 1484. After her death (1468), he undertook major military campaigns conquering western Asia up to the Euphrates River. He allied himself with the Mitanni.

Upper Egypt southern Egypt with the desert area and the elongated, narrow and fertile Nile Valley. The southerners were more isolated and conservative than the residents of the delta. A king from Upper Egypt probably conquered Lower Egypt around 3000 BC.

Ur Sumerian city-state which constituted a centralized empire in Mesopotamia from ca. 2100 to 2000 BC. Ur assumed the dominant position of Lagash. The Sumerian renaissance is called the Ur III Period after the successful third dynasty in Ur.

ushebtis Egyptian figurines serving as funerary equipment in addition to food and other objects. They were supposed to perform the tasks which were given to the deceased in the kingdom of the dead, e.g., answering questions posed by the gods.

Valley of the Kings western bank of the Nile opposite Thebes where the New Kingdom's pharaohs were buried. They were placed in wooden human-shaped mummy cases in burial tombs hewn from the rocks. The royal funerary temples were built separately on the shore of the Nile.

vizier high Egyptian administrative official, usually a close relative of the pharaoh. He controlled the levying of taxes, the lower officials, the court and the royal treasuries, and granaries. Like other officials, he was buried in a *mastaba*, a rectangular decorated grave near the pyramids.

wanax a Mycenaean ruler. He was commander of the army and the administrative officials, and he owned much land which he rented out in part. In his palace the administration was kept for land use, manufacture and trade, agriculture, the artisans, and industry. Most likely these rulers were independent but in contact with one another.

ziggurat Sumerian temple tower built on terraces. It was decorated with stylus mosaics, whereby colored styluses were affixed to the clay temple walls. The temples played a central role in the life of the Sumerians.

Bibliography

Ancient Egypt
Aldred, C. *Egyptian Art.* London, 1980.
Baines, J., and Málek, J. *Atlas of Ancient Egypt.* Oxford, 1984.
James, T. G. H. *Pharaoh's People: Scenes from Life in Imperial Egypt.* London, 1984.
Lichtheim, M. *Ancient Egyptian Literature*, 3 vols. Berkeley, Los Angeles, London, 1973-1980.
Málck, J., and Forman, W. *In the Shadow of the Pyramids.* London, 1986.
Spencer, A. J. *Death in Ancient Egypt.* Cambridge, 1992.

The Minoan Civilization
Buchholz, H.-G., ed. *Aegäische Bronzezeit.* Darmstadt, 1987.
Buchholz, H.-G., and Karageorgis, V. *Prehistoric Greece and Cyprus: an Archaeological Handbook.* London, 1973.
Castleden, R. *Minoans: Life in Bronze-Age Crete.* London, 1992
Dickinson, O. T. P. K. *The Aegean Bronze Age.* Cambridge, 1994.
Myers, J. W., Myers, E. E., and Cadogan, G. *An Aerial Atlas of Ancient Crete.* Berkeley, 1992.

Mycenae
Chadwick, J. *Linear B and Related Scripts.* Berkeley, 1987.
McDonald, W. A., and Thomas, C. G. *Progress into the Past: The Rediscovery of Mycenean Civilization.* Bloomington, 1990.
Sachermeyer, F. *Die Levante im Zeitalter der Wanderungen: vom 13. bis zum 11. Jahrhundert v. Chr.* Wien, 1982.

The Sumerians
Kramer, S. N. *The Sumerians.* Chicago, 1964.
Oates, J. *The Rise of Civilization.* London, 1976.
Parrot, A. *Sumer.* New York, 1961.
Postgate, J. N. *Early Mesopotamia: Society and Economy at the Dawn of History.* London, 1992.
Roux, G. *Ancient Iraq.* Harmondsworth, 1972.
Woolley, C. L. *The Sumerians.* New York, London, 1965.

Akkad and the Sumerian Renaissance
Kramer, S. N. *The Sacred Marriage Rite.* Bloomington, 1969.
Kuppers, J. R. *Les nomades en Mesopotamie au temps des rois de Mari.* Paris, 1957.
Oppenheim, A. L. *Letters from Mesopotamia.* Chicago, 1967.
Postgate, J. N. *The First Empires.* Oxford, 1977.
———. *Early Mesopotamia: Society and Economy at the Dawn of History.* London, 1992.

Hammurabi and Gilgamesh
Heidel, A. *The Gilgamesh Epic and Old Testament Parallels.* Chicago, 1976.
Lambert, W. G. *Babylonian Wisdom Literature.* Oxford, 1960.
Oberhuber, K., ed. *Das Gilgamesj-Epos.* Darmstadt, 1977.
Saggs, H. F. W. *The Greatness That Was Babylon.* London, 1962.
———. *Ancient Near Eastern Religion.* London 1995.
Sandars, N. K. *The Epic of Gilgamesh.* Harmondsworth, 1970.

Babylon
Jacobson, T. *The Treasures of Darkness: A History of Mesopotamian Religion.* New Haven, 1976.
Lambert, W. G. *Babylonian Wisdom Literature.* Oxford, 1960.
Oates, J. *Babylon.* London, 1979.
Oppenheim, A. L. *Ancient Mesopotamia.* Chicago, 1964.
Saggs, H. F. W. *Everyday Life in Babylonia and Assyria.* London, 1965.

Assyria
Andrae, W. *Das wiedererstandene Assur.* Munich, 1977.
Cardascia, G. *Les loi assyriennes.* Paris, 1969.
Contenau, G. *Everyday Life in Babylon and Assyria.* London, 1954.
Laessoe, J. *People of Ancient Assyria.* London, 1963,.
Mallowan, M. E. L. *Nimrud and Its Remains,* 2 vols. London, 1966.
Oded, B. *Mass Deportations and Deportees in the Neo-Assyrian Empire.* Wiesbaden, 1979.
Saggs, H. F. W. *The Might That Was Assyria.* London, 1984.

Further Reading

Boyd, Anne. *Ancient Egyptians.* New York, 1981.

Brown, Dale, ed. *Mesopotamia: Land of Empires.* Alexandria, VA, 1995.

———. *Mesopotamia: The Mighty Kings.* Alexandria, VA, 1995.

Cheney, David M. *Son of Minos.* Cheshire, CT, n.d.

Fleming, Stuart, *The Egyptians.* New York, 1992.

Foster, Leila M. *The Sumerians.* Danbury, CT, 1990.

Harris, Geraldine. *Ancient Egypt.* New York, 1990.

Hart, George. *Ancient Egypt: Three Thousand Years of Mystery to Unlock and Discover.* Philadelphia, 1994.

Healy, Mark. *The Ancient Assyrians.* Mechanicsburg, PA, n.d.

Macaulay, David. *Pyramid.* Boston, 1975.

McLellan, Elizabeth. *Minoan Crete.* White Plains, NY, 1976.

Oates, Joan C. *Babylon.* New York, 1986.

Pearson, Anne. *Everyday Life in Ancient Egypt.* Danbury, CT, 1994.

Reeves, Nicholas. *Into the Mummy's Tomb: The Real-life Discovery of Tutankhamen's Treasures.* New York, 1992.

Sauvain, Philip. *Over Three Thousand Years Ago in Ancient Egypt.* New York, 1993.

Illustration Credits

Index

Text is indicated in roman type; illustrations are indicated in italic type.

283

Text is indicated in roman type; illustrations are indicated in italic type.

285

Text is indicated in roman type; illustrations are indicated in italic type.

Text is indicated in roman type; illustrations are indicated in italic type.

Text is indicated in roman type; illustrations are indicated in italic type.